What Readers Ar

and T

"The Girl in Your Wallet definitely lives up to its back cover description. I will not only recommend the book to my friends and colleagues, but to the many others challenged by addiction and incarceration."

—**GHEORGHE TURCIN**, Reentry Specialist,
Washington State Dept. of Corrections

"Nickell tells the story of her long road through addiction and abuse in this inspirational debut memoir…. It's a remarkable story, overall–not just because of what Nickell went through, but also because of what she was able to achieve: She owns and operates a highly profitable bakery business. Nickell speaks of God often, but she also discusses the psychological work that she put in to improve and forgive herself, making this a useful book for both religious and secular readers. A stirring account of a hard life and hard work."

—*Kirkus Reviews*, reviewing this book's first edition

"I sourced Teresa as a guest speaker as an SBDC business advisor. Her ability to connect with multi-industry participants on many topics was engaging and offered insight into small business owners' daily realities. After reading her amazing book, I knew her transition into teacher and coach was inevitable."

—**KIRK DAVIS**, MBA, Executive Director, Center
for Advanced Manufacturing Puget Sound, Former
SBDC Advisor, Green River College

"Teresa is an amazing communicator and able to hold her audience as she delivers a compelling message. She is a woman of character and is excellent at leading group discussions, involving the audience, and facilitating conversations. I highly recommend her and am confident she will inspire every audience she speaks to."

—**SHARON REDDING**, Director of Women and
Children, Seattle Union Gospel Mission

"I had the pleasure and privilege of featuring Teresa Nickell as a guest speaker at Seattle Revival Center (SRC). Teresa skillfully articulated her story with poise, grace, and confidence. Her delivery and choice of words painted a vivid picture and the presentation made very clear her dedication to Women's Prison Ministry. Her concluding request to support this cause was unquestionable."

—**ABIGAIL O. EDWARDS**, Founding Member, SRC Women's Ministry

"You'll find no self-pity within these pages! Teresa is transparent, humble, and strong. I learned many things to apply to my own life as I read her story. I can't say enough about the value of this book and the solid honesty Teresa poured into it. Read it. You won't be sorry."

—**DIANA KILPATRICK**, Author of *Off the Record* and *When Mountains Don't Move*

"At first glance, most would never know this put-together business woman had a dark past of incarceration. Not only was her story extremely relatable to the female inmates, but the women walked away with a living example that anyone can turn their life around no matter where their past has taken them. Teresa was easy to work with and flexible in her presentation. At the last minute, our presentation time got cut, which allowed only a short window for our event with no flexibility. Teresa had her message prepared down to the minute."

—**GREG FULLER**, Field Director, Prison Fellowship, Washington and Alaska

"I have known Teresa for more than ten years now...but never knew the real Teresa I learned about in her book. In working with her as a consultant for her business, I know Teresa as a competent, successful business leader and owner. She was always very confident in her abilities and now I know where this confidence came from. She has overcome a lot to accomplish the success she's had in her life. This book is perfect for anyone whose successful future is being derailed by family, addiction, or legal issues from the past and who wants to learn how to overcome them to live a happy, successful, and purposeful life."

—**GRANT ROBINSON**, Owner, People Values

"I knew Teresa for fourteen years as a successful business owner but never knew the depths from which she arose, the abuse she faced as a child, the resulting demons that haunted her, and the lifestyle that many would discard as a wasted life. Teresa is living proof that people who appear lost to addiction can be saved. This book may motivate you or someone else to seek help that could save a life."

—**GREGORY HAFFNER**, Principal Attorney, Curran Law Firm

"From prison to ownership of a multi-million-dollar company, Teresa Nickell's story is one of insights, inspiration, and hope. Her message prompts readers to break free of self-limiting beliefs and take the steps forward that lead to ultimate freedom."

—**PATTI COTTON**, Executive Consultant, Coach,
and International Fortune 500 Speaker

"This book is an honest, gripping, and courageous memoir. If you want to break free from the guilt, regret, shame, and self-destructive thoughts that are holding you back, then read and reread this book!"

—**PATRICK SNOW**, Professional Keynote Speaker and International
Best-Selling Author of *Creating Your Own Destiny* and *Boy Entrepreneur*

"Life can be extremely hard at times, but in The Girl in Your Wallet, Teresa Nickell shows us that the journey is all worthwhile. She has been to hell and back, having survived damaging relationships and debilitating mistakes, and experienced incredible growth that has allowed her to heal her inner child and become a woman who inspires others in their own growth. Don't miss the opportunity to experience and heal through the magic in these pages."

—**TYLER R. TICHELAAR, PHD** and Award-Winning
Author of *Narrow Lives* and *The Best Place*

The Girl in Your Wallet

Teresa Nickell

The Girl in Your Wallet

2nd edition

ISBN-13 (print book) 978-1-636180540

Library of Congress Control Number: 2020925646

Soli Deo gloria

Cover design by O'Daniel Designs

Printed by Gorham Printing in the United States of America

Published by:
Aviva Publishing
Lake Placid, NY 12946
518-523-1320
www.avivapubs.com

Address all inquiries to:

www.TeresaNickell.com

To my fellow sisters who remain in bondage.
What happens to you matters to me.

CONTENTS

SECTION THREE · Where I Am Now

Healing the Broken Places

PREFACE

I CARRY A PICTURE in my wallet of me as a little girl. I'm about four years old, wearing a pretty dress and a bow in my hair. The black-and-white photo, tattered and worn, is very old. I carry it with me to remind myself to show compassion to my younger self. She didn't deserve what happened to her, nor did she understand it. What she went through should never have happened. What she should have had eluded her. She was confused, scared, and just wanted to be held. None of those things were available to her. She lived in a world where children were unseen, unheard, and didn't do much of anything right. Why was I wearing a dress? I don't know, but it would've been very unusual. It also must have been a special day because we rarely went to Grandma and Poppa's house. But there it is in the background.

When I reach into my wallet, I see the little blonde girl with her hands clasped in front of her. She's innocent, confused, isolated. In my mind, I see her lifting her arms to block blows to her head. I remember grieving for the childhood she didn't get to have and weeping for her losses and loneliness. But as with all grieving, it had to end. She and I have now made our peace, and we are no longer waiting for the past to change. We are in this life together for the long haul, looking with hope toward the future. Time and time again, I have silently reassured her that I will be the adult she needed then. I will be the one who will show her kindness and compassion when she's scared. She is always with me, in me. She gets acknowledgment from me that she has value, that she matters, and that she is loved.

I think of that little girl, and I am proud of her. She survived things she didn't understand, and that caused her pain. She maneuvered in ways that allowed her to make it through. She mustered the intellect and the survival instincts of someone much older. She prevailed.

I understand now that the thinking patterns developed so early in my life no longer serve me. I must challenge what I believed was the truth when I was young. That perspective was based on my limited view and processing abilities at such a vulnerable age. That little girl's decisions ruled my life for a very long time. We got into some trouble, she and I. We learned to manipulate and influence others. Behind this manipulation was an endless, desperate need to figure out ways to defuse angry situations. Often, we were frantically just looking for a place to hide or flagrantly just wanting what we wanted!

The little girl is still fighting for control. When I see her in my wallet, I'm reminded to challenge those thoughts that are so instinctive. I have learned to pause because those thinking patterns were developed by a scared, confused child who always felt like she was twenty minutes late to the movie. She was playing it all by ear. She didn't understand the outside world, nor did she trust it.

I see her often in my wallet. I remind her that she matters, that I will always care for her to the best of my ability, but that she's not calling the shots anymore. We need grown-up decisions made with grown-up wisdom. She responds best to structure, but she has very little skill at creating it, and, in all honesty, most of the time, she just needs to be told no.

INTRODUCTION:

PULLING BACK THE CURTAIN

"He didn't open the gates of heaven and let me in.
He opened the gates of hell and let me out."
— Heard at an Alcoholics Anonymous meeting

YOU MAY NOT know why you're here, but I do—you're tired of destructive, self-limiting beliefs holding you back day after day. Or, perhaps, you have been trying to help someone else and have exhausted all your best ideas. You want someone to reignite the hope that you can unload the weight of guilt, regret, or shame. You've picked up the right book. The process won't destroy you, and I can prove it. I will go first.

Let's start with a few questions. Do you stay busy because spending time alone allows the memories to creep in? Do you have a game-face for everyone else, but an honest look in the mirror is far more difficult and revealing? Are you driven to overachieve because anything less might reveal your insecurities, and other people will discover you're an imposter? Exhausting, isn't it?

I was the successful owner of a multi-million-dollar corporation on the outside, but inside, I carried an image that replayed incessantly in my mind—I'm staring at myself in the bathroom mirror. The crack cocaine had long been burned, but I couldn't put the pipe down. I had scoured the floors on my hands and knees for the imaginary rock I had dropped, picking up fuzz and hearing it sizzle as I dropped it into the bowl of the pipe. I could not look away from my reflection in the mirror. Hating myself, tears streaming down my face, yet unable to put the lighter down, I could not stop. Could. Not. Stop.

My fingers were burned, having held the lighter for so long, and I was at least a day late in picking up my child from the babysitter. My reflection cried at the hopelessness and deplorable behavior. That is the girl I could not forgive. I accepted I was an addict, but somehow, I maintained the idea that I should have been able to beat it. I can see now that it is ridiculous, but I held a grudge against myself. I referred to that era in the third person, more specifically in terms of how much I hated "her." She was weak, and I was angry and ashamed of her.

As I was polishing up my outside for work and hating "her" simultaneously, I was also unknowingly waging war on others. I was harming relationships with my coworkers, sabotaging my career, and pushing away those who loved me the most. I couldn't stop because I didn't understand why I was doing it. Those are decades I will never get back. I hope you won't wait as long.

I have heard that guilt demands punishment, and for me, that was true. I made progress on this healing journey a little at a time and was not always aware that I was growing. When I was aware and felt unfamiliar moments of joy, the image of that horrendous thing I had done, participated in, or even masterminded would pop into my head. Guilt told me I was beyond redemption and that I deserved to be in pain. I began to understand I had to deal with the source of that guilt.

Discovering the driving force behind my actions and a good mentor was vital. This book is written in an interactive format to help you get to know yourself in a new way. I will share my life events, good and bad, and nothing is off-limits. I am quite literally an open book. I won't give you a set of steps to take or rules to follow. I will share the steps I took. It's up to you to decide what is useful. Don't give up if the content gets a little uncomfortable. Stick with me. I will bring you through the actions and thought processes I took to get from where I was to where I am today—peaceful, fulfilled, and content. I will share some ideas on how to find a mentor. I also hope you will consider seeing a counselor or therapist to keep the growth going.

After what I consider twenty-nine years of therapy, including Alcoholics Anonymous, Al-Anon, counselors, therapists, personal Bible studies, and church services, I have been blessed to sit under the direct teaching of two of the country's best-known Christian psychologists and authors on multiple occasions. I have reached the point that I can reflect on the past without reliving its pain. This manuscript in no way encompasses everything I have experienced and received healing for or what I'm still working on. The work continues.

It was suggested to me many years ago that I should stop comparing my insides to everyone else's outsides because I will always find myself lacking, but it took a long, long time for that to sink in. You'll likely notice that I often address the women I work with in prisons and shelters, and I hope they feel the inclusion. I hope we all make it.

"Do not be afraid; you will not suffer shame. Do not fear disgrace; you will not be humiliated. You will forget the shame of your youth and remember no more the reproach of your widowhood."

— Isaiah 54:4 (NIV)

Some might say I've shared too much detail in this book, but it doesn't change my position. Early in sobriety and Christianity, I searched high and low for someone to reveal the depths from which they had been saved. I listened to the testimony of a former motorcycle gang member who left his life of crime. I read the account of a former prostitute. Their stories of redemption were touching, and clearly, they too had participated in behaviors they deeply regretted. Even so, because they glossed over their sins, I still believed mine were worse and possibly unforgivable.

Are you ready to begin and put the past behind you for good this time? Now is your time. If I can do it, you can do it. I believe in you, so let's lock arms together, with me as your virtual mentor. Allow me to help you make the rest of your life the best of your life—letting go of guilt, regret, and shame, and making room for God to work in your life.

Your friend,

Disclaimer

AS I PREPARE TO OPEN the vault of my memories and put them into words as I see them, I realize I can't tell you my story without relaying portions of other people's lives as I perceived them. I have changed the names of several to protect their privacy. My goal is to be accurate in telling my story, not defamatory, prying, or mean-spirited in describing the people who played a part in that story.

This book contains the truth, as I understood it, through the eyes of who I was at every point in my life. I'm sure these events will be remembered differently by the others involved, but I cannot speak for them. I can only share my recollections, perspectives, opinions, and beliefs. When I describe others' thoughts, motivations, or desires, I am sharing how they appeared to me. Only they can fully tell their own stories.

Every effort has been made to source all quotes properly.

SECTION ONE

What My Life Was Like

CHAPTER 1

Beginning Innocent

"In order to move forward, you have to look back."
— Matt Maher

I WAS BORN IN 1965 to a troubled young couple who already had two sons. My father was an alcoholic of the most violent kind. I have very few early memories of him. My mother was scared, submissive, critical, and sarcastic. The best legacy they could offer me was mired in violence and alcoholism. I lacked positive role modeling.

My parents had a volatile relationship, to say the least. My father beat my mother when he was drunk. He carried a rage that, when alcohol was added, became uncontrollable. He was always drunk or hungover. Being the youngest, I may have suffered the least from it. I have limited memories. My two older brothers may tell a different story.

"Grave emotional damage" would be an understatement, although we have all handled it in very different ways. My siblings and I are not close. They don't understand me and the life I live today. I have moved on. While hardly unscathed, I am happy, and for this, I am grateful. I made it out, for the most part.

My family's shame and embarrassment began in a small house on a dirt road on the south side of Spokane, Washington. We lived next door to one of my dad's friends, Bud. Bud was a biker who also painted cars and motorcycles in the shop he had behind his house. I didn't know anything about painting cars, but I knew everyone talked about what a good job he did, and he supported himself that way. As children, we three kids didn't have many friends in the neighborhood, and I'm certain it's because of the dysfunctional and illegal behavior that was going on in our home. I am also sure that other parents in the neighborhood didn't encourage their children to play with us. I can remember the awkwardness of walking to and from school twenty feet ahead or behind small groups of other kids, some of whom even lived on my same street, and never being asked to join them. In all fairness, I didn't try to either. I had learned my place as an outcast very early on.

"Little Tinkerbell" was what the adults called me. "Hey, Tinker, grab me a beer!" was what I heard most often from the bikers in the backyard. They'd be spread out on the lawn, listening to loud music from a rock station on speakers strung from inside the house, their rows of motorcycles lining the backyard. Although my dad didn't have a bike of his own, these were his people, and by association, they were my people. I have no idea if they were affiliated with a motorcycle gang, but I know they weren't doing toy runs for children's hospitals. It was not uncommon to wake up and find a couple of "leftovers" from a party the night before passed out in the yard, sometimes with their bikini-clad girlfriends next to them. We walked over them on our way out the door to school. It was a tough crowd. I remember a bizarre little man called Rabbit crouched down in the backyard with a dirty, wadded-up rag clutched in his hand. I have no idea what was on the rag, but I know that when he would put it up to his nose and inhale, his eyes would roll back in his head, and he would fall over into the fetal position. There was also Bob, who had lost an arm from hopping the trains. With his empty shirt sleeve billowing in the wind under his scraggly beard, he was very scary. Some days when walking home from school, I would find my dad in the middle of the street, pounding his fists into my mother's face. I always had anxiety my entire walk home, but especially when I was about to round that last corner because I had no idea what would be waiting there for me.

I felt socially awkward and still have some social anxiety. I have developed a pretty good "game face," but it can be very tough once I run out of small talk. Never having allowed anyone to get too close can create a great deal of loneliness. It would be years before I could see that plenty of people had tried to get to know me in the past and that without even knowing it, I had pushed them away. I had developed protective responses that were so instinctual I never even saw them.

I once heard a woman describe herself as always feeling like she was "twenty minutes late to the movie," and boy, can I relate. That was me! I was certain everyone else had life all figured out and that there had been some sort of orientation and education I'd missed. I was always on the outside looking in. She said something else that depicted my family in those days, "We lived in a poor neighborhood, yes, but our neighbors were poor; we were trash." That described us—high drama, violence, and chaos. The police driving slowly by our house was a regular occurrence. These were the role models I had as a young child. I learned about male superiority as men talked down to their wives and girlfriends. I learned about drug and alcohol dependence from addicts who took no responsibility for their actions. I learned that there was always someone to blame, be it the government or someone else. I learned my station in life. I understood that when two men disagreed, there was going to be a fight. I was taught that police were to be feared; only bad people (like us) carried guns. We were all just born on the wrong side of the tracks, poor and disadvantaged. We'd take whatever we could to get by however we needed to do it.

My mother was most certainly a victim and played the role well and often. She taught me that a woman's worth was based on her ability to attract a man, any man. She was small, cute, and fun. Her conversations, however, were based on how she looked, dressed, and whether guys showed an interest in her. Since my dad was often drunk early in the day, this gave her plenty of time to be the life of the party. I never understood how she could participate in the alcohol and drug lifestyle and not partake of the actual substances. To the best of my knowledge, she didn't even dabble in them. What she desperately craved was attention, which she perceived as love.

As children, we learned how to stand in food bank lines and acquire government butter and cheese. We were coached to say all the right things at the food bank, to lie to get what we wanted or needed. I remember my mother telling us that our dad sold the turkey we got at the food bank for a case of beer. I always wondered why she felt it was important we knew that; she can still bring it up today, more than forty years later. Women did not get pregnant. They got knocked up. Most of the time, it was implied that they did it on purpose to trap the man as an act of vengeance. Children were a burden.

My mother was truly victimized. There's no question about it. What she did with the situation was something I would despise, and to my utter horror, repeat. She learned how to be a victim and milk it for all it was worth. It was not something she did intentionally, nor did I. But when you desperately need affection and care from people and don't know how to ask for it, being a victim works. She was seeking love from people who were just as lost as she was. I don't remember my mother ever giving me a hug or an affectionate pat. Words of encouragement were just not spoken. As I grew into adulthood, I would realize that nobody had ever given her any either. Turns out, hurting people hurt people.

I am not sure where my mother learned to be so critical of everyone and everything. Perhaps it was from the nuns in the Catholic school, of whom she spoke so poorly. Maybe it was her mother, a bitter woman, who passed it down to her. Maybe both. She was highly critical. "With a sharp tongue" doesn't begin to describe the way she could cut us down. We could do nothing to her satisfaction. Negative narrations were given every step of the way. Discipline could include withholding food or clothing. It proved impossible to comply when the expectation for what was good behavior was constantly changing. We never knew what would provoke her. We didn't have any actual conversations in my childhood home. You know, ones where one person speaks, you listen, and then you have a chance to speak. We learned we had no added value.

Here are some of the phrases I heard a lot: "Pick that up. You're a pig. How stupid do you have to be? That's ridiculous. You'd be better off not thinking at all. Do you call that clean? That's just filthy!" My all-time favorite conflicting messages from my mother were, "You'd better lose a few pounds if you think any guy is going to want you," followed by "You're not leaving that table until you clean your plate. We can't afford to waste food."

Which was it? Eat or be thin? I learned that nothing I did or didn't do would ever satisfy her goal because the goal changed daily, sometimes hourly. I simply was not good enough then and was never going to be. So why try? I was too young to experience any self-pity about it. It simply was the way it was. I learned to stop trying to please her and accept that I would always be a burden to our people and society. It was best to keep to the shadows lest the verbal battery be taken public. Public ridicule was the one arena I could avoid most of the time because we were always in hiding. However, insults and put-downs were just her way of communicating. This type of communication was not saved solely for us kids, but was the way she also spoke to her husbands.

I do have a couple of sweet memories from those early years. One evening, one of my dad's biker friends asked my mom if it would be okay to take me home for the evening to his house out on the lake. (Don't cringe. He was a nice man.) I went with him, and it was a big adventure for me. I still remember him rowing me out to the middle of the lake in the morning because I said I wanted to go swimming. But I never got out of the boat. He was a very kind, gentle man whom

I will always remember fondly. As I've grown in my relationship with the Lord, I look back and realize now that there must have been a motive for him to show me kindness, specifically on that day. I suspect he was aware there was evil lurking around me and did what little he could to protect me, if only for one day. Twenty-five years later, as I was preparing for work, the Holy Spirit would prompt me to write him a thank you letter. The thought was so powerful and repeated in my head so often that I had to stop what I was doing and do it. Six months later, I received a very short card in return. It was written in several different colored inks, obviously written one sentence at a time at several different sittings. It must have been very difficult for him to write. He wished me well and noted he was glad to hear that I turned out okay. Less than two months later, I would get the news that he'd been killed by a drunk driver while riding his motorcycle. Had I not responded to the urging of the Holy Spirit that day, taking those ten minutes and being a little late for work, he might never have heard the words "thank you" from a child he had showed kindness to that day so long ago. I have learned when the Lord asks me to do something, I need to respond with a sense of urgency, with haste. It may be my only opportunity to do so.

We had a Sunday night ritual of baths, pajamas, and Walt Disney. I remember the tender touch of my father, brushing out my wet hair as I sat on the floor in front of the TV. It is the only time I remember my father touching me affectionately.

My mother flirted with the guys while my father was in the other room, in the backyard at the party, or passed out. If you think your young children aren't paying attention and learning something when you are behaving recklessly, you are wrong. I was observing her every move: the hushed voices, the slight giggles, the hand up the back of her skirt I saw when I walked into the kitchen. I still remember this image of my mother, especially since this happened at eye level for me. Over and over, I learned that a woman's value was based on a man's desire for her. She would go on to have many relationships, never ending one before entering another. She was always the other woman, the affair, a pattern she would repeat throughout her life. She had mastered the ability to attract a man but lacked the ability to be a good and loyal wife. She was just as critical of the men in her life after she married them as she was of her children.

We lived in a communal house at one point, meaning several families in a very large, old house situated in the middle of a manufacturing district. It's hard to say how many adults there were, but there were about ten kids and a couple of dogs. The second floor was one large room, and that's where we kids spent our time. We were either herded upstairs with the door shut behind us to play or go to bed, or herded out into the yard. We all came downstairs to eat at the table at the same time and then went back upstairs or outside. To the best of my knowledge, we lived on welfare the entire time we lived with my biological father. He was in and out of jail, and when he was out, I don't remember him ever working. I don't remember being taken to a single visit to the dentist or receiving any other medical care, other than the required vaccinations to go to school and a visit to the eye doctor for my bad eye.

I had an underdeveloped or lazy left eye. I wore Coke-bottle glasses and a patch for a while, trying to strengthen it, but to no avail. This didn't lend itself well for fitting in with the other kids. It was just one more example that I wasn't good enough. Strangely, I have no memory of the kids taunting me. I wonder if it was because I lived in "The Scary House."

I began learning the deeply rooted thinking that my opinions and feelings had absolutely no value. I was simply along for the ride. I hid a lot to minimize my presence. There's a familiar adage that children should be seen and not heard. For my siblings and me, children were not to be seen either. I accepted that my opinion and presence were simply not important. Even more than that, I believed that the "good" and "important" people of the world made the decisions, and the rest of us just had to live with them. Crazy? Maybe, but true, nonetheless. I also learned the unspoken rule that I could do whatever I wanted so long as I didn't bring the authorities home—no teachers, principals, or cops. If I went unnoticed by outsiders, I was left alone by my people. For a time.

My mother has never been able to communicate her feelings. If I asked her questions about more sensitive topics, she completely shut down. For example, when I came into womanhood at the age of twelve and asked her what I should do, she hurried away in a flutter and said, "Ask your girlfriends; don't ask me," and went on to excessively clean something. She hasn't been able to share any life knowledge or experience with me. So, I observed life on my own and made decisions, never confident I was handling them correctly.

My maternal grandmother had given birth to three children by three different fathers—scandalous in the 1940s. She didn't raise any of them in her own home. They all attended and were boarded at the Catholic school. My mother had been raised in a Catholic school until she was eighteen. I only remember my grandmother as very short with us, snappy with my mother, and generally unpleasant. When we visited her, I was seated on the couch and given a Sears catalog, expected to stay silent until it was time to go.

While snooping through my grandmother's drawers one day, my mother discovered the man she had believed to be her father all those years wasn't related to her. She would search out her birth father, only to learn her mother had divorced him while he was overseas in World War II and then lied to her about it.

My father's parents lived on the south side of Spokane. My paternal grandfather seemed to be generally happy most of the time, and we had a very superficial and sporadic relationship. There was no getting close to that man, although he was delighted to play his organ and banjo while singing, "When the Saints Go Marching In."

My paternal grandmother ruled the roost and was bigger than life. It was very clear she did not like my mother, and although she was nicer to us, she clearly had a distaste for us kids. We didn't often visit, which is why the photo in my wallet is so unusual. It would be decades before I learned the root of that hostility. It was due to my mother having an affair, this time within the family.

Study Guide

The Girl in Your Wallet

Chapter 1: Beginning Innocent

What do you think I meant when I wrote, "I made it out, for the most part"?

____

____

____

What circumstances do you find yourself in that you would like to get out from under?

____

____

____

Was there a "scary" house in your neighborhood, whether in childhood or adulthood? What made it scary?

____

____

____

Many of us received good messages mixed in with some painful ones. These may have even come from people outside of our immediate family. What are some good messages you learned that have served you well?

Which negative messages from your childhood might be holding you back?

Do you and I share any experiences? Which ones could you identify with the most?

CHAPTER 2

Overlooked

"I just wanted to be someone, to mean something to anyone."
— Charlotte Eriksson

MY DAD AND his friends used to go down to the train yard and hop onto empty train cars to get wherever they wanted to go. I'm not sure of the details of how all that worked. I just know one night that's where he and his friend Jim went. It was around 10:00 or 11:00 p.m. when my mom woke up one of my brothers and me. We packed up everything we could carry and left in the dead of night. That was it. No explanation. She said, "Shut up and do what I tell you." We went to an apartment in the Spokane Valley where we moved in with my dad's best friend, Jim, who showed up the next day. No explanation, no reasoning. Where was my other brother? I was told it was none of my business and to stop asking questions.

Early on, my brother and I knew our mother was the desirable one, and we were simply baggage. What happened to my oldest brother is still a mystery to me. For whatever reason, he went to live with the biker, Bud, next door at the old house. He could not have been more than fourteen or fifteen. This would begin to make sense to me in my forties, but I'll have to get back to that later.

My brother and I were expected to act like this was the family unit we had always had. I still remember my confusion when my mom and Jim went to bed in the same bedroom together. I can still conjure up the shock of it all. I can still see my young self, staring down the hall, lost in space and time. I always draw a blank at the mentality that "because I said so" somehow made it all understandable and acceptable. We would soon be registered at a new school and coached on what short story to tell anyone who asked. We had just moved to the area. Say no more.

The hardest part of my carrying out my role in my mother's lies was the lack of guidance. We were told what to say and what not to say. But since the conversations never played out like her coaching sessions, I sometimes didn't answer on the fly. My teachers assumed I was developmentally disabled to some degree and started speaking more slowly to me like I didn't understand. I just didn't want to get in trouble for saying the wrong thing, and I didn't have the confidence to know what that would be.

The one lingering memory from living in this apartment building was finding a rusty razor blade lying in the parking lot. I crouched behind the building and dragged it along my skin, back and forth, barely cutting the top layer of flesh, not drawing blood, but mesmerized. It seemed to have me in its control. Or maybe I felt powerful holding it; I am not sure. I smuggled it into my bedroom and kept it hidden in a small box—my little treasure.

Somewhere around my twelfth birthday, I received an AM/FM radio as a gift in that apartment in the valley. What a cherished gift! If I turned up the volume high enough, I didn't hear the screaming. My mother had left the man who had beat her, but it hadn't made her happy. She and Jim argued quite a bit. That radio further instilled in me my lifelong love of music. I immersed myself in listening to it. The artists and their song lyrics became my only friends. I loved listening to Sunday morning radio with Casey Kasem and hearing the stories behind the music. Music provided great therapy for me and still does. I connect with the emotions and experiences of the lyricists. Not only did it drown out the yelling coming from the other rooms, but it also opened me up to a whole new world full of adventure. With all the parties at our house, I loved music as far back as I can remember. I spent my time with that radio, trying to decipher every word to every song. These artists became my friends: The Who, Bad Company, and Crosby, Stills, Nash, and Young. I devoured every album cover sleeve to learn the lyrics and the history of the band members. What adventures they had! To this day, I can take it especially hard when a favorite musician passes away. Thinking about the death of Ronnie James Dio still makes me sad. I have had people ask me how I could be so upset at the passing of someone I have never even met. I tell them we have been friends for years.

I don't remember the actual sequence of many events throughout a lot of my life. One of the only ways I've been able to determine when a life event happened is by remembering what new song was on the radio at the time. Odd, but true. I can tell you I was ten years old when my mother left my dad because "Philadelphia Freedom" was new on the radio. I can tell you I was home attempting to raise my son in 1985 because Guns N' Roses hit the radio at that time. I know I was doing methamphetamines in 1990 because Metallica and Nirvana had their biggest hits. Music was the only constant I had in my life since I always had the radio on. It has been the only way to pinpoint any kind of timeline to my life before 1992.

I was probably thirteen when we moved into the house where I would stay for the remaining days I lived with my mother, my brother, and Jim. It was located in the Hillyard neighborhood of Spokane, and although it was a decent, older house, it was in the lowest income part of the city. It was the kind of place you joked about yourself before other people did it for you, kind of in the same way heavy people make fat jokes about themselves because they think you might. We lived in the hood. Big deal. That's where people like us lived. Ironically, there actually were multiple train tracks in Hillyard, and I spent a fair amount of time on the other side of those tracks. It was the poorest of the poor, crime-ridden, and I was fascinated by it. My self-esteem was nonexistent. I felt I belonged there. We will go where we feel accepted.

Jim and his friends actively did drugs, smoked pot, and did hallucinogens, and they never tried to hide it. They also drank a lot of beer. Sometime when I was around age thirteen, they began to offer it to my brother and me. First, it was smoking pot, and then they gave us mushrooms and acid (LSD), I am sure solely for their entertainment. As the drugs kicked in and we began to hallucinate while watching TV, Jim and his friends sat chuckling on the couch behind us. I didn't care, and neither did my mom. By her logic, we were going to do it anyway, so it may as well be in the safety of our own home. At this point, I was elated to have found some means of escape to kill the emotional pain I felt inside. These drugs offered me an escape from reality for a time, and I welcomed it. The problem for me was how to make the escape last longer. The numbing effect always eventually wore off, and the pain was still there waiting.

I imagine puberty itself is difficult enough, but I wouldn't know. Dealing with a home life such as mine, I am guessing, made it even tougher. I didn't fit in anywhere, and I lacked social skills. I don't remember the classes I took in school. I don't remember ever doing homework. I do, however, remember the first time I drank alcohol. Or I should say, the first glass. I blacked out from the first drink, remembering nothing, which continued for my entire drinking career. I can't recount the number of times I woke up not knowing where I was—or who I was with, for that matter. No shoes, no purse, and having no idea how I got there. It happened often. That was how I lost my virginity, somewhere around age fourteen. No memory of it at all—just waking up knowing it had happened.

With alcohol, I lost all inhibitions and became an entirely different person. I proved to be a promiscuous young woman, although I have limited memories of it. Alcohol made me feel beautiful and accepted, and I was looking for love. I was confused about why these boys never wanted anything to do with me again until the next party. I had yet to understand the difference between the girl a guy wanted to sleep with and the girl he was interested in really getting to know. Since I had not yet witnessed a healthy relationship, how would I know? I was mimicking my mother's behavior, but I wasn't getting her results.

I sold pot at school for my stepfather. Jim would roll me eleven joints per bag. I sold them for a dollar a piece, and for every ten I sold, I got to keep one for myself. I was in eighth grade at the junior high school. I would get up early and go first to the high school because it started earlier. There, I would sell what I could in the parking lot and then walk down to my school and sell what was left. I was popular with a certain crowd of kids, which was a big deal, given how hard I was trying to belong somewhere. But as soon as I didn't have any pot anymore, they didn't want to hang out with me. I was valued for what I could do for them, not for who I was.

Then Jim suffered a terrible accident at work. He worked for a swimming pool manufacturer, and when a crane broke while lifting a swimming pool mold, it landed on him. I don't know the severity of his injury, but he was lucky to have survived. He was flat on his back for at least four months. He always had large bottles of pills on his dresser, and when he was able to get up and move around and leave the bedroom for a while, I started dipping into his prescription pain pills. I never really liked them because they made me nauseous, but I was just looking to kill my emotional pain. They worked in a pinch. It was better than nothing. I was willing to try anything at that point.

Jim was confined to home for a very long time and was heavily medicated. My mother worked at the candy factory up the street and was gone all day until dinner. There were several hours between when I got home from school and when she came home, hours that would become a living hell for me. If you remember where

Jim came from, he was not the most respectable man. He may have been a step up from my dad, but that did not make him honorable.

One day, I came home from school to find Jim in a hostile fervor, frantically running around the house, breaking my mother's things. All the doors were open, and I tiptoed through the house, not sure what I would find. I just knew something was off. What I did find was a bathtub full of water and bleach and all my mother's clothing. Jim was ranting and raving, and when I asked why, he said, "If your mother had any sense, she would've hidden her birth control pills better. I have had a vasectomy."

My mom was having an affair with a coworker. For a long time after that, she wore those bleached-out clothes. It was a mark of her shame, much like the giant red A the woman in Nathaniel Hawthorne's *The Scarlet Letter* wore on her chest to signal adultery. My mom and Jim's relationship never recovered, although it still took some time for them to separate. It was about to get much worse for me too.

As I was developing into a young woman, Jim took notice. When I came home with a hickey on my neck, he asked me if I was giving it away, why couldn't he have some? There were comments, looks, and propositions, and then he started exposing himself to me. I suffered sexual molestation in my own home by my stepfather, for what I could only guess was about a year. His program was to list every mistake (real or perceived) I made over time, and then I could choose. I could allow him to touch me and keep his secret, or I could let him whip me on my bare skin with his leather belt. The choice was mine. I chose the less painful option, as he knew I would, not knowing it would be the longer-lasting hell. Because he had a plan and a goal of his own to meet, there was always something on the list, multiple things I had "done wrong." These included fabrications, exaggerations, and anything in between. He made sure he found things for which I had to be punished. What I understood was that by simply existing, I was bad. There was no way out. I was swinging wildly out of control, surviving just on plain rage and an ever-growing addiction. I was shutting down and becoming numb. Then a switch went off inside me. I had tried to be good and please people in every way I could possibly imagine. One day, I thought, *They're never going to be happy anyway. If I'm going to be called bad, I'm going to show them bad.*

One day, my eldest brother stopped by our house, which he occasionally did, and found me up in my room crying. As I sobbed, I blurted out what had been going on. He was furious and went downstairs shouting. In a million years, I would've never guessed what happened. My mother called me downstairs, called me a liar, and told me to get out of her house. I was fourteen.

Study Guide

The Girl in Your Wallet

Chapter 2: Overlooked

I described the impact of traumatic loss when my mother left my father in the dark of night. What did I lose that evening?

What losses did you experience in childhood? List one or two events that come to memory more quickly or more often.

Can you remember being told to "Shut up," or being told "It is none of your business," or being left out? How did it make you feel? Does reflecting on the memory make you still feel that way today?

Children are often introduced to adult themes when very young, before they can have a complete understanding of what is going on. I witnessed drug use and was offered drugs at a very young age. Were there people in your life who introduced you to adult themes far too early? Who were they? How did that affect you?

I was elated to have found a way to escape emotional pain. In what ways have you tried to cope with emotional pain? (Example: shopping, new relationships, etc.)

Music is a strong trigger of memories. What are some songs that trigger memories for you? What do they bring up? (List at least one happy memory!)

CHAPTER 3

Going It Alone

"Where there is anger, there is always pain underneath."

— Eckhart Tolle

AFTER LEAVING MY mother's home, I slept in a series of places. They call it couch-surfing nowadays. Well-meaning people would take me in for a day or two, sometimes a week. I would sell them on my sad story, but I misused their kindness so they quickly tired of me. I was an angry, dishonest young woman who rummaged through their belongings when they weren't home, ate their food, and left the mess. In my defense, I didn't know when I would get to eat again. I don't clearly remember stealing, but I know I must have. I was intensely bitter! I turned my rage outward on neighbors and teachers without ever speaking the words out loud. Why didn't they come and save me? I resented anyone whom I perceived had a better life than I did, and I believed that was everyone. My homelessness landed me in multiple places a young woman of fourteen should never have been. I never told anyone my age, and I am sure they thought I was much older. A schoolmate who talked her father into letting me stay with them for a while ran with a little bit different crowd. I experienced my first den of intravenous drug users. I was both mortified and fascinated by what I was watching. I was mortified because of the absolute scariness of what I saw—the needles, the blood, the vomiting—and fascinated because I was certain the user was feeling no pain, and I was in a lot of pain. My friend, who was just starting down this path, was obsessed with the hypodermic needle, playing with it, fondling it. If there was nothing else to put in her veins, she would shoot up sugar water.

Somehow, I managed to complete the tenth grade, although it took four or five different schools to do it. Continuation high schools were where rebellious, difficult children were sent as a last-ditch effort. The truth is, I don't remember much about it. My attendance at that point had been sporadic anyway, and they placed far less emphasis on attendance in those days. I could pass the tests, so they moved me forward. It was a lack of address that became the problem, and I had no one to sign my notes from the teacher. One of my greatest regrets is dropping out of high school after the tenth grade. A part of me died as a result. I would have recurring dreams for years about trying to find my classroom, books, or locker. I love to learn and always have.

The hardest part about this period was understanding where the hell my mother was in all this commotion. What was she thinking? She sat silently by, cleaning obsessively, acting like everything was fine when I visited her. Everything was not fine. I carried a rage for my mother that lasted thirty years. I was furious that she hadn't made better decisions in her children's best interest. Fury, and I mean complete rage, consumed me and showed up in all my interactions. Tripwires were everywhere. I exploded on many unsuspecting souls. Did my mom even consider us? Why in the world did she even have children?

Years later, much to my horror, the reality would prove that I would follow in her footsteps. I didn't make better decisions. I didn't know I had the power to make my own decisions. I learned to behave in the same way I had been shown, no matter how much I hated it.

Eventually, I went into foster care, although I have no idea how I arrived there. I couldn't have entered the system without some authorization from my mother or the courts deeming me uncontrollable, which was another curious example of how easily she could give her children away. I was out of control and surviving on just plain rage and active addiction.

Another attempt to control me or make the problem go away was when I was sent to live in Toledo, Oregon, with my maternal great-aunt and uncle. Geography changed nothing. Everywhere I went, my anger, dishonesty, and raging alcoholism came along.

The high school in Toledo was very small. I showed up in my heavy makeup and tight clothes and with my foul mouth. It's not hard to imagine why I didn't fit in. I made sure my classmates rejected me. I also drank the booze in my great-aunt and uncle's house and refilled the bottles with water. I did not last long in their home. All of this was before my sixteenth birthday.

My mother ended up moving in with the coworker with whom she had the affair. I don't think he was physically violent, but he had a completely unreasonable temper. I only met him a couple of times.

To say my view of marriage or even a healthy relationship was normal could not have been further from the truth, and I followed suit according to the examples I'd seen, completely oblivious to the fact that I had a choice in any of it. The baffling, recurring theme of my life was truly believing I had no choice.

Finding Acceptance

In my early teens, I found some solace, friendship, and unconditional love with a group of local kids, most of them like me. They came from dysfunctional homes of their own. We were outcasts and hung out in the local park. Although none of them possessed the power to change their circumstances or mine, these kids would become my family. We didn't talk about our troubles; we just tried to experience some level of happiness and joy, most of which came by way of alcohol and hallucinogens. After long nights of drinking, we spent many early mornings combing cow pastures, searching for mushrooms.

The beautiful thing about this group was the ability to wander in and out of it freely without any jealousy or difficulty. We shared a camaraderie, a common bond. We would branch out with different kids to do other things with ease, even pairing up intimately, and there was never any jealousy. We didn't feel bitter for having been left out of something because nothing was ever planned; life happened at the spur of the moment. All we had was the moment. Everything happened spontaneously and immediately, and, of course, almost everything had to be free. We went where we were accepted. We had little money, and if we did have any, it was spent on cigarettes, beer, pot, or gas. Our activities revolved around these things. That included who hooked up with whom. Looking back, I can't see how we avoided jealousy around this issue. I only know we did. Remarkably, no one got pregnant. Not that I know of anyway.

At some point, I landed in a group home facility that housed numerous other misfits. We all had a story. I remember receiving some new clothes, which was noteworthy because it had never happened before. I am not clear where they came from, but I was happy about it until some other damaged young woman stole them. At this home, I learned about a Job Corps program that taught life skills and provided room and board to young adults. You had to be sixteen to enter the program, so after my birthday, I left to go to the Job Corps in Yachats, Oregon. This is my only indicator of how old I was at the time.

Tasting Success

When I arrived at Job Corps, I was given a choice of what training I wanted. I chose the culinary arts program and began working in the commercial kitchen, feeding 200 other participants and staff. It wasn't long before I worked my way into the small bakery in the back of the kitchen. I spent much of my free time on Saturdays in that little bakery. I loved to bake! Without the substances that gave me courage, I was still very shy. But I was excelling for the first time in my life.

My stay at Job Corps marked the first time I had stopped using drugs or alcohol since I was twelve. They gave me a bed, meals, and structure, which I liked very much. I attended school and work. I had set times to be at both, and they clearly explained that I would lose privileges if I did not keep the schedule. I showed up everywhere on time and participated fully. I felt good about myself and was proud of my work. I was enjoying hearing positive feedback from the adults, although it made me uncomfortable at first. This was all very new to me. Job Corps relit my desire to learn. I had stability I had never experienced before, clearly defined expectations, and continual coaching and feedback. It took a while to assimilate. This strange new world was confusing, but I wanted it. I learned to speak up and asked questions, carefully testing this and closely watching for my instructors' irritability. They simply answered my questions and carried on. My long-established anxiety had a brief reprieve in this environment. I could breathe.

Then, I met a boy.

Study Guide

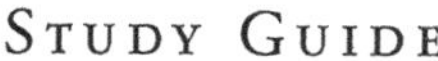

The Girl in Your Wallet

Chapter 3: Going It Alone

Anger is seldom the primary emotion. There is always some other feeling the anger is hiding. I describe it as "Tripwires were everywhere. I exploded on many unsuspecting souls."

What "hot button" issues of your own have you identified? If nothing comes to mind, consider if others have mentioned any difficulty they have when communicating a particular topic with you.

___

___

___

It makes no sense at a conscious level that I was in a new school, being offered a fresh start and "made sure they rejected me." Describe a time when you may have sabotaged your success.

___

___

___

With my friends in the park, I found solace, friendship, and unconditional love. Where did you seek out acceptance and friendship in your youth, if only for short periods? What were the results?

___

___

___

I was doing well with the structure and positive feedback Job Corps provided but abruptly changed direction. What happened to change my course? Fill in the blank below. What is the last sentence from Chapter 3?

Then, I ______ a ______.

Describe a time when you abandoned a course for a similar pursuit.

CHAPTER 4

Seeking Shelter

"Children who were abandoned grow up to love people who abandon them."
—R. H. Sin, *Planting Gardens in Graves*

IT WAS AT Job Corps that I met the first man I would marry, Curtis. He told me I was beautiful and that he would take care of me and protect me. He was the first man who ever wanted to be around me sober. I was no longer invisible. He listened to my opinions. We were both sober most of the time in Job Corps. There were isolated times when alcohol would be smuggled in, but for the most part, we were clean. He truly saw the real me, and that had never happened before. He was strong and demanded respect. I fell for him. He protected me. No one would mess with me while I was "his old lady." As I look back, I can see glaring signs that he was not good for me. He was just like the men I had observed in my youth. I took comfort in that.

When Curtis had completed his minimum time to earn a leave into town, we planned a weekend. Things started well until alcohol was introduced into the scenario. We started drinking, and violence ensued. The next thing I knew, I was being admitted into the local small-town hospital with a black eye and for overdosing on speed. The

Job Corps staff retrieved me the next day, and I was given a second chance. When asked what had happened, I honestly couldn't answer. I could only say I was sorry and assured them it wouldn't happen again. The truth was I didn't know what had happened. I had yet to understand my condition. I was just happy Curtis hadn't found me unforgivable, and we were still a couple.

I stayed in the program for a total of nine months, attending school to obtain my GED and Basic Culinary Arts Certificate. Applying myself diligently, I succeeded in getting both. The center director called me into his office, asked me about my plans, and urged me to reconsider leaving with Curtis. He pleaded with me to stay and let this guy go. Of course, I thought he was crazy. Why didn't he understand? No one else wanted me. No one ever had. I couldn't miss this chance. My only chance!

I had just turned seventeen when I got off the Greyhound bus in Tacoma, Washington, to meet Curtis in his hometown. He told me he had come from an alcoholic home with a violent father. We shared an understanding of each other. It turns out I was looking to marry someone just like my dad, and I was successful. He, too, was a violent man, and it allowed me to continue being the victim I had been taught to be. Black eyes, fat lips, and sprained ankles were common occurrences. Most of the physical damage would eventually heal, but the emotional damage, heaped on top of the negative load I was already carrying, would further kill me inside. Curtis also appeared to believe my body was his playground. I loved him, and I hated him.

Curtis and I began our distorted relationship in 1982, sharing a home with another couple. The woman had been in Job Corps with us, and the man was a friend of Curtis's. It was a time of heavy drinking and crazy, wild living. In the middle of all this spin, I conceived. His friends would ask me, "What are you doing with this guy?" and I always wondered what they meant.

In April of 1983, when I was seventeen years old and three months pregnant, Curtis and I were married. I cried through our entire wedding night, living through what he deemed his rights as my husband. He suggested it was my wedding gift to him. My mom had signed away her rights to me and given legal guardianship to Curtis, who was twenty-one. It is important to note the cruelty I inflicted on him as well. I must own that. My motto was, "You hurt me, and I'll hurt you back." That meant physically (yes, I hit too) and emotionally. Later, during my fourth step of Alcoholics Anonymous, I would retrace my actions during this time. I'll share more of this process later in the book.

Naïve as I was, I had no idea what was happening to my body as the baby began to grow. Curtis's mom worked on the maternity floor of the hospital and tried to help me learn about pregnancy, childbirth, and breastfeeding. God bless the woman for her endurance and caring, but I was upset that I couldn't drink. Drinking, not my pregnancy, was truly what was on my mind. I tried to drink a few times but, after a couple of sips, became terribly sick. Because I couldn't drink, Curtis left me at home a lot, which worsened my anxiety attacks. When I did go out with him, I could see how his demeanor was developing throughout the evening and somewhat predict what his behavior was going to be. I could then modify my behavior to try to manipulate the desired outcome, namely that the evening would not end in my getting hurt.

On nights when Curtis left me at home, I felt anxiety and panic because I had no idea which Curtis would be coming down the street and crashing through the door. Would it be the gentle man greeting me with a big hug and telling me he loved me? Those moments were rare, but they did happen. Or would he fly down the street, park sideways in the front yard, stumble in the front door, and pass out? Those were more frequent. I would peek out the curtains all night long, afraid he would come home in a rage, ready for battle, looking to take out his frustrations. There were also times when he wouldn't come home alone, and I would be forced to smile and socialize with women he had picked up at a bar or somewhere along the way. Sometimes I was told to stay in the bedroom and be quiet, which I, of course, did—while steaming, jealous, feeling sorry for myself, and helpless.

The first baby shower I ever attended was my own. For that matter, the first baby I ever held was my own. I knew nothing about babies. In my childhood environment, children were not celebrated. They were something a woman "did" to a man to tie him down. But I fell in love with my child!

My son was born in September of 1983, two months after my eighteenth birthday. We named him Christopher. Because my mother-in-law worked on the maternity floor of the hospital, I received a great deal of kindness from staff and the midwife she knew personally. I was a scared, just-turned-eighteen-year-old girl who had not read any of the material given to me about what to expect. I had predetermined that I just wanted the drugs. It was really no choice for me at all. Killing the pain had been my motto my entire life. The phrase "going natural" was ridiculous to me. In my extreme naiveté and youth, I also could not grasp why they urged me to breastfeed. I was finally able to drink again. Why would I do something to prohibit it?

When I went into labor, Curtis drove me to the hospital and was in the room with me most of the day. I recall him sitting in a beanbag chair watching cartoons and telling me to stop acting like a baby. I would later hear him tell the story about what a beautiful event it was, that he was there for his son's birth, and that he cut the umbilical cord. I remember it a little differently. In fact, when he got close enough to me, I took a swing at him. After the birth was over, Curtis took off to meet his cousin to celebrate. Others would later tell me he went out partying with a couple of strippers. I was heartbroken, alone, and felt betrayed. But this was my normal way of life, and to be completely honest, I thought I deserved it.

My role in the family was to access every program available to low-income people, and I was effective. We received welfare help in cash, food stamps, and medical benefits. I knew how and where to trade food stamps for money and how to fence stolen goods. I was a regular at the pawnshop. We worked the system in every way imaginable. Curtis almost always had a job, but I had elaborate schemes to keep the scams going despite that. He was talented in all areas of construction and mechanics and made good money. What seemed difficult was holding a job. Payday would result in a binge that sometimes lasted for days. Then, sadly, we would not be able to afford the rent, utilities, or food, and sometimes not even gas for the car.

By the time I was twenty-two, I had been in court twice for welfare fraud. While I'm grateful I was never convicted, I certainly could have been. The central theme of my frame of mind during this entire time was always the same. It was Curtis's fault, whatever "it" was. He made me lie to the state. He made me lie to the utility company. He made me lie to the landlords. The reality was my training had begun long before, in those early food bank lines, being coached by my mom about what story to tell.

I became so competent at playing the victim; I still find it unbelievable. I sold my sad story to people every step of the way. While I most certainly was a victim, I milked it for all it was worth. I would bring up reasons people should feel sorry for me: he hits me, we don't have any money, we don't have any food. I'd watch the body language of the person I was speaking to so I could assess how my story was being received. I would then use my observations to manipulate that person, hoping to arouse pity and get what I wanted.

A major obstacle for me in sharing some of my life's events with you is my discomfort when well-meaning people hear my story and say, "I'm so sorry" or "How terrible for you." I spent decades hoping to get people to say those words, and today, it saddens me. No consoling me is necessary. I am not suffering. I'm not that person anymore.

Should we ever meet, please do not tell me how sorry you are. As I mentioned in the introduction to this book, my purpose in sharing as much detail as I have is to clearly display no hole so deep that God's arm can't reach down and pull you out. I was in that hole, and I hadn't seen the light in a very long time. Sharing any more details than these serves no godly good.

Despite the physical, emotional, and sexual mistreatment, I loved Curtis deeply. He took care of me and paid attention to me more than I'd ever experienced before. I was no longer invisible. I was fiercely protective of him. I would lie to the police, landlords, and the welfare office to protect him. I would engage in a physical battle to protect him from harm. I don't pretend to understand the psychological reasons for why I was willing to defend him regardless of what he was doing to me. It had its own twisted logic based on emotion.

Further, in the deep reaches of my mind, I think I might have been more responsive to those trying to help me if they understood how much I loved him. Well-meaning people would see I was beaten and bloody, and I would say what a piece of crud he was, but when they agreed with me, I became angry. I would turn on them when they spoke poorly of him because I loved him.

In my insanity, I abused myself as well. I jumped out of a car going thirty-five miles an hour, I jumped off a second-story balcony, and Lord only knows what else. We lived crazy lives, and I believed I deserved to be in pain. I understood pain. I did not understand happiness. There were many visits to the hospital during this time, yet I can only pinpoint three of them. God has allowed me to remember what those three visits entailed. One was for cracked ribs, a broken nose, and a black eye. The hospital staff wouldn't let Curtis in the room with me, but the police did come. I kept up my story, whatever it was. Usually, I said I fell down the stairs, walked into a door, or something of that sort. They never believed me and told me they knew what had happened and I didn't have to live that way anymore. They had run his arrest record, but they didn't understand he was all I had. No one else wanted me. I had nowhere else to go.

Curtis would ask me why I couldn't just stand there and look good. I thought that was a compliment because I was pretty. It also reinforced my belief that I was stupid, that nothing I could say had value, having been told as much since I was a kid. He was just the next in line to remind me of my inferior social standing. Then, there was also a sweetness after a violent episode. He became very tender, very gentle, and often shed tears of regret. He would tell me how sorry he was, telling me he would be more careful in the future because "you're my favorite toy. If I break you, you won't play no more."

Another hospital visit was to have glass removed from the thumb of my right hand. We had been at a house party, and I thought Curtis was in a fight in another room. I charged my way toward the action, but a guy tried to restrain me, presumably to stop me from getting hurt. I was drunk and violent, and I hit him in the face with my beer mug. Rumor had it that he received fifty-plus stitches on his left cheek. I became further disgusting to the people in that circle, and they turned me into the police. I didn't go to jail for it because the defendant didn't attend the hearing. The memory of hurting someone else like that has been very difficult for me in my journey of forgiving myself and believing God could forgive me too. I still can't bend my right thumb because my tendon was severed that day, and I seriously harmed an innocent person whose injury would be visible for the rest of his life.

My third visit to the hospital was due to the physical toll the excessive alcohol had on my system. I'd had numerous bladder and kidney infections by this time. They were so severe they required medical attention in a hospital setting. My body was suffering severe wear and tear years before the substance abuse would end.

Curtis was often in and out of jail, but I don't think there was ever a charge for assaulting me. These were the days when the woman (me) could deny what happened, and the police had to take her word for it.

I was grateful when the law later changed to state that if a domestic violence call was made to the police, one person was sent to jail.

I left Curtis repeatedly. I convinced myself he was the source of all my problems, so I wandered home to Spokane somehow with the sympathetic help of some caring soul who heard the story of how cruel he was. When I arrived and realized the misery I had left behind in my family of origin hadn't changed, I would be back with Curtis in just a couple of days. The panic about how I would survive would set in. I had never worked and had no money. I needed him for a place to stay and protection. It was a trade-off I understood and accepted.

My drinking was escalating, and I was suffering the effects of it. Numerous times I would "wake up" in the middle of a conversation and not know how I got there or what we were talking about. I wasn't just having blackouts from drinking. I was having memory blackouts when I wasn't. It happened while I was visiting an old friend. I felt very uncomfortable because I couldn't remember how I'd gotten there or if the last time I'd seen her, she was pregnant. I was filled with anxiety when she finally said, "Aren't you even going to ask me if it was a boy or girl?" I tried to fake my way through it and failed miserably. I'm sure I came off as not being very intelligent most times, but I simply could not remember. I was certain I was losing the use of my mind.

It was like I was drowning in a body of water. I was flailing about, and as I would briefly surface and look around, I would have only a moment of understanding where I was and what was going on, then sink back below the surface.

I had no idea who the president was, nor did I care. I can't verify many events' chronological order throughout the years of my drug and alcohol use. There are things I know with certainty. I just can't tell you at what point they happened. Remember that while my memory of something seems solid, the interpretation of it is also through the mind of someone unstable, angry, under the influence, and paranoid. Since I only had my thoughts to rely on, no matter how distorted they were, to me, they were the truth and either propelled me forward or held me back.

Curtis expressed a desire to have many, many children. And while I was not allowed to have an opinion, I felt we were unfit parents. I can remember three abortions. There may have been four. Seriously, I cannot tell you for sure. All I know is he was actively trying to get me to conceive (which I did), and I would sneak off and "take care of it." His mother gave me a maternity sweat suit for my birthday one year and whispered in my ear that she had left the tags on it in case I decided "not go through with it." I didn't.

You may ask what happened to the baby? I loved my child deeply, but I had no idea how to take care of him. My mother-in-law, sister-in-law, and grandmother-in-law all offered every bit of help and support they could, all of which were taken for granted. Looking back, I see that I viewed their kindness as a means by which to milk them for money and babysitting. I cannot imagine the terror and distress that Curtis's family had as they watched our attempts to be caretakers for our infant. We loved Christopher with all our hearts. We had plenty of love. What we did not have was knowledge, stability, and anything resembling kindness in our home. Nor did we have supplies. I could give plenty of examples of poor parenting, and not being able to care for my child was just one more nail in the coffin. I'd even paddled him too hard a few times, also because hitting was what I knew. Not only was I a failure at everything I'd ever tried to do, but I'd also failed this infant.

Christopher's Nana, his great-grandma, cared for him virtually every weekend. Picking Christopher up on Sunday turned into picking him up on Monday, which turned into picking him up on Tuesday. Eventually, his grandmother sought custody when he was four years old. I couldn't care for Christopher and the thought of dragging him through the things I was exposing myself to sickened me. How could I ever get him to school? My addiction overpowered everything. I was a lost cause, but someone wanted him. Both Curtis and I agreed with his mother that it was a good idea she take custody, so we each signed legal custody over to her. From then on, Christopher lived in her safe and stable home.

Curtis and I had many public displays of violence, but many more of them were in private. Unless there was an eyewitness, we made up stories of falling downstairs, tripping over a rug, or even having a fistfight with one of my girlfriends, and the stories were believable. Of course, when Curtis was making the excuses, I agreed, nodding my head at all the right times, even with the black eye, missing hair, or a split lip. The irony was that I would provoke him relentlessly into hitting me. That smart-mouth I developed would be used to poke at him, throw insults at him, and embarrass him in front of other people. Being in public was the only place I felt I had power. It was crazy the cycle we went through. I can only imagine it was because I craved those periods of regret he had when he showed me great compassion. It was a trade-off I accepted.

In at least two instances, police officers stepped in and took me into their protection. With our lifestyle, the police were around us all the time. One time they kept me in a motel overnight until I had somewhere else to go where I'd be safe. To me, no such place existed. I stayed the night, but where was I to go? Where would I be safe? In the morning, I went back home. A second time they took me to a battered women's shelter. Again, my thought process was, "What am I supposed to do? You don't understand! I cannot live on my own." Beyond that, I didn't want anybody to harm him. I would do that crazy thing in my mind that prompted me to cry out, "Save me! Save me!" But the second anyone physically restrained Curtis or caused him any perceived harm, I would lose my mind to protect him. It was a no-win situation. No one could help me but myself. I just didn't know it yet.

Alcoholism escalated to cocaine addiction, and then snorting cocaine escalated to freebasing. I would cook it up over the kitchen stove in little glass vials and smoke it in glass pipes until my eyes rolled back in my head. Remember that weak eye from my childhood? Well, I would get so loaded that the eye would bury itself in the corner by my nose, making me extremely cross-eyed. It was very uncomfortable, and it freaked other people out because I looked so messed up. People gave me a lot of trouble about it, so I simply taped a patch over my eye and kept going.

When crack cocaine became available, it sure saved a lot of time, trouble, and money. We no longer needed a house and a stove to cook it up, but I had to go to bad neighborhoods to get it. Along the way, the progression led to "crank," more commonly known now as methamphetamine, or meth. Once I discovered meth, my drug exploration ceased. I had found my drug of choice. This was the substance I'd been searching for my entire life. I had arrived. I felt alert and alive. My normally agitated and nervous behavior lessened.

During this time, my sinuses became terribly infected from snorting this drug. I had no idea where the drug came from, who made it, or what was in it. Green snot started running uncontrollably from my nose. Since stopping using was never a consideration, I went to the health food store, bought empty capsules, and began to fill them with the drug and take it orally. I found I could take a larger quantity by ingesting it, and I always needed more. I had to find a way or make a way to consume more.

We lived in nine different places over four years, sometimes living in unfit homes and sometimes being evicted for abusing the property. I only know this because I managed to keep a reasonably good baby book for my son where I documented every one of our addresses. Toward the end of our time together, Curtis and I lived in an abandoned, old, single-story apartment in a rural part of South Tacoma. I should say I lived there, and he visited, coming around to sleep for a couple of days and then taking off again. I had plenty of company since our entire circle of acquaintances needed somewhere to hide out just like I did. They talked a nice neighbor into running a garden hose from their house to flush the toilet. We used kerosene lanterns for light and spliced into someone's phone line for service. We would pick up the telephone quietly and listen for a dial tone to make sure we weren't interrupting somebody's call. We could only call out. I think we were there about four months, but there's no way I can be sure.

While in this place, my smart mouth got me into some long-lasting trouble. I was lying on the floor when I said something I thought was funny at Curtis's expense, trying to embarrass him in front of the crowd. He threw a Bic cigarette lighter in my direction to startle me. Unfortunately, I chose that moment to turn around, and the lighter hit me at full impact in my only good eye. The pain was immense. I was immediately blinded, seeing nothing but bright, white light, whether my eye was open or closed. I was screaming! I had never experienced that level of pain before.

Loss of vision impacted my life terribly. I lost nearly all my sight because I only had 20/200 vision in my other eye. Essentially, I lost about 85 percent of my eyesight. I could see well enough not to walk into walls, but I could not read or see any kind of detail. Colors and shapes, that was it. I could only tell quarters from nickels because of the ridges on the edge of the quarter. It chills me to the bone to think I drove that entire time, not only without clear vision but also under the influence and with no driver's license or insurance. Thank you, Lord, that I never harmed anyone.

I had to look at my marriage certificate and my divorce decree to calculate how long Curtis and I were legally married—eight years. But my next relationship melded so seamlessly into the one with him that I barely remember even going to court for the do-it-yourself divorce.

When I met Curtis, he had a partial tattoo on his arm, and I suggested what image he could create with it. He took my idea and spent the rest of our relationship reminding me we were forever bonded by ink. He didn't write my name in his flesh, but he might as well have. I can still hear him mocking me, saying he was the only one who would decide when our relationship was over, ever reminding me of my powerlessness.

Chapter 4: Seeking Shelter

At our core, we all want to be known, seen, and accepted. Did this new person in my life seem like a safe place to reveal my most intimate self? Why or why not?

I understood the conditions of my relationship with Curtis and that they were "a trade-off I accepted." What do you think the difference is between a compromise and a trade-off?

My frame of mind during this time was constant. Nothing was my fault. I was good at playing the victim. What is the difference between being a victim and playing a victim?

I have openly given you a window into the mind and thoughts of an addict living in the disease's progression. I was taken to a women's shelter, given a hotel, and even left Curtis on my own to go to my mom's house in Spokane to get away. What type of thinking always brought me back to him?

Have you seen this thinking in yourself, friends, or family? How did it play out?

Going blind, being beaten, losing custody of my son, and being arrested was not enough to bring me to seek help. As friends and family of addicts and others, where do our influence and responsibility end?

Does this awareness about addiction help relieve any guilt or shame you may be carrying for another person's life? How?

CHAPTER 5

Misplacing Trust

"The story will repeat until you get it."

— Nitya Prahash

IN OUR EARLIER years, I felt loved by being the sole focus of Curtis's obsession, but eventually, he tired of me and went looking for the next big adventure. I also wasn't the shiny trophy I had once been. The wear and tear of this lifestyle and its high toll on my physical body were showing. There were newer, fresher models attracting his attention. One day, he left me at a drug dealer's house and told me I had better not leave until he came back. Huddled in an empty room on a cold floor with nothing but a blanket curled around me, I stayed in that drug house for what must have been a week. Not having any money of my own to support my habit, I did the cleaning and tried to be helpful in exchange for whatever dope they might share with me.

As I was cleaning one day, one of the guys struck up a conversation with me. A nice man, he asked me if I would come to his house and clean it for him if he paid me. Without so much as a second thought, I left with him. His name was Mark. He had a gentle spirit and quiet demeanor unlike anything I'd experienced before. He was very kind, but all the red flags were there. Moving forward with Mark was a bad idea from the start. I was so worn down by that time, though, that I felt the fact he even wanted me around was like winning a prize. He was better than the last one, so he must be good, right? Mark would become my second husband, but it would be a while before that happened.

Mark was a very gentle man, very different from what I had ever experienced before. He showed me kindness, gave me a place to stay and food, and we shared a similar lifestyle. He was a very private person, but as we got to know each other better, we realized our childhood experiences had caused us both a great deal of pain. Although our experiences were different, the results were the same: shame, regret, and anger. He seemed to understand my need to squash emotional pain.

This relationship, of course, worked for me. We were evicted from his apartment shortly after I moved in. In this case, it was completely due to not paying rent, which had never been the sole reason for eviction in my previous experience. As I mentioned, Mark was a very gentle, soft-spoken man, but he also made it clear from the beginning he was not looking for a relationship. I would not be his primary focus. He would ask his neighbor out on a date within my line of vision as I waited in the car. I said nothing, thinking in time I could win him over. Mark's detachment from me would not change over time. I never did "win him over," although he seemed to become more enamored with me when I later began to make more money in my job. I can see now I confused his attention with love. He seemed pleased when I continued to make and spend more money, and he put pressure on me for more. Even then, I would not be his main concern.

One of the negative beliefs I carried from my past into my relationship with Mark was that if a man truly loves you, he will hit you. My first marriage had further reinforced this. So, I did everything I could to aggravate Mark to the point of violence. A behavior I understood, but viciousness simply was not in him. After a time, I stopped provoking him and stopped flinching when he walked by me. For that, I am grateful to him.

I continued in my drug use until one fateful day in early 1991 when the police kicked in the door. I wasn't home at that exact moment, but as I drove up the long driveway of our apartment complex, I knew something was very wrong. When I pulled into the parking space, a neighbor girl came running out of her apartment to tell me the police were there. In a split second, a very large man dressed in black ripped the groceries from my hand, slammed my face against the pavement, and held me there with his foot on my head. It all happened so quickly. Chaos ensued, and I was handcuffed and brought into my apartment, where I sat across the room from a handcuffed Mark. As the police rummaged through our things, I tried asking Mark questions by mouthing the words. He could understand what I was asking, but I couldn't see him well enough to understand his replies. I honestly had no idea what kind of trouble we were in. I had always been able to talk myself out of trouble and thought this time would be no different. I was wrong.

We were driven away in a nondescript white van, my desperate little dog chasing us down the driveway. To this day, it brings me to tears that I couldn't take care of him, the same way I couldn't care for my child. What an absolute failure. I was charged with possession of a controlled substance with intent to deliver (sell) and possession of stolen property. Apparently, there were also stolen credit card numbers in our apartment used to purchase power tools and other building supplies, likely for their resale value. I don't say that with any finger-pointing. I simply didn't care to know about it. All I cared about was that my needs were being met. I had drugs to use, a place to sleep, and a man to make all the decisions for me.

I had no realization of the severity of what was going on. I was still high—my normal state. I thought I would get booked into jail, and I would talk my way out of trouble, the way I always had before. I also believed the fantasy that Mark would be let go. I didn't yet know this was not his first brush with the law.

The arresting officer, the one who had slammed me to the ground, waited for me after I was transported and booked into jail. In a moment of compassion, he said he was sorry he was so rough with me. He explained he had been shot at, stabbed, clawed, and kicked in the balls in his job. He'd had a prostitute spit in his mouth. He never knew what he was going to encounter or if he would make it home each day. He told me, "Today, my job was to subdue you, and I did my job. If I had known you were going to be this gentle, I wouldn't have treated you so harshly. I am sorry it went down this way, and I hope you're not too sore tomorrow." I have always appreciated his visit.

Jail itself is a scary proposition. Entering the facility's cell area, I saw someone had written above the door, "Welcome Back." The sign must have been reasonably large since I could read it. Passing the other direction through the same doorway, someone had written, "See You Soon." I suppose there's a lot of accuracy to those statements, but they sure didn't give me very much encouragement.

I was twenty-six when my misdemeanors became felonies, and I entered the Pierce County Jail as if it had a revolving door. After booking, I was shuffled to a bare concrete room where a female guard had me strip down completely for a search. I was handed a jail uniform, mat, sheet, and pillow and was pointed to a spot on the floor. After all my years on the streets, I thought I was tough. I quickly learned all I had was a smart mouth. These women were tough, and I was afraid of them.

Chapter 5: Misplacing Trust

There were many red flags in my new relationship. How did I reason moving forward? (Fill in the blank.)

"He was _______ than the last one, so he must be ______, right?"

Mark clearly stated he was not interested in a relationship. I admit I heard the words but interpreted them as a personal challenge. What did I believe I had the power to do? Was I successful?

____

____

____

Have you believed you could make someone do something in your own life? What was the outcome?

____

____

____

What belief/behavior do I credit Mark for helping me overcome?

____

____

____

What painful situations can you look back at to see the lesson they provided?

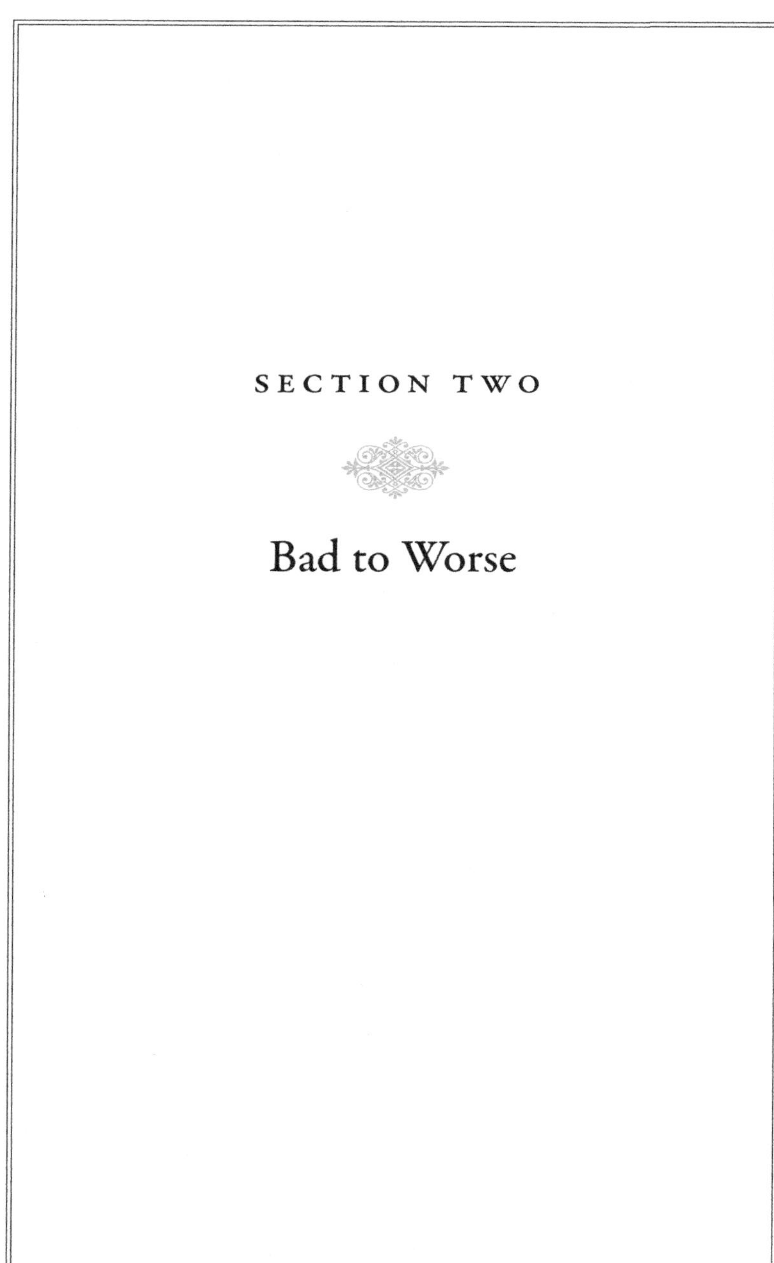

SECTION TWO

Bad to Worse

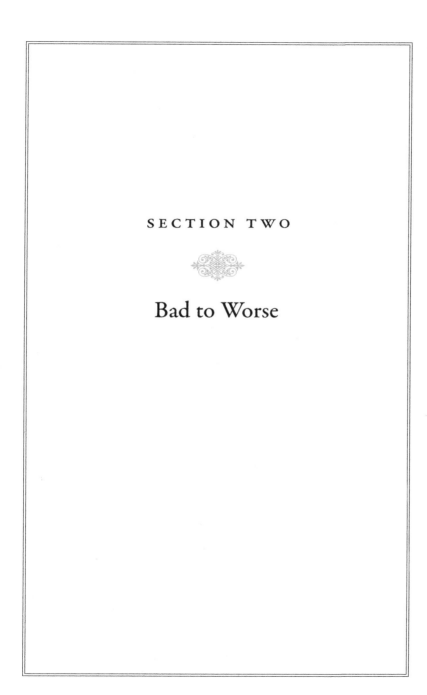

CHAPTER 6

Reaching Rock Bottom

"No one saves us but ourselves. No one can and no one may. We ourselves must walk the path."
—Gautama Buddha, Saying of Buddha

IT TURNS OUT the worst day of my life and the best day of my life were the same day. Going to jail was the event that forced my hand. I could no longer talk my way out of the consequences of my actions.

The following day, shackled to a group of women, I shuffled in front of the judge for my arraignment. I have no idea the amount of my bail. The only thing I remember is being confused by the charges and told I qualified for a court-appointed attorney. I was still so strung out that none of it made any sense. It was about the third or fourth day in jail that I gained a little mental clarity and suspected they weren't going to let me out of there just because I said I was sorry. I did my time of 35-45 days, trying to go unnoticed, and did reasonably well. Because it was my first offense and I had no criminal record, they dropped the credit card fraud charges and the intent to deliver. I was formally charged with possession of a controlled substance (methamphetamine), a felony.

My mother contacted the bail bondsman on my behalf and put up the title to her home as collateral for my bail. She drove over from

Spokane, a four-hour drive, to pick me up when I was released. I wanted out of jail, but I was overcome with dread that she was taking me back to that horrible place, a childhood from which I'd been trying to escape my entire life. When the elevator door opened on the jail's bottom floor, I took one look at her in the parking lot and took off running the other way. I had nowhere to go. I just kept running.

Although Curtis and I were no longer together, he gave me an old beat-up Dodge Valiant with a broken window. I have no idea who really owned it, but I was grateful to have somewhere to sleep out of the rain. The bucket seat on the passenger side wasn't bolted down, and I was small enough that I could take it out and huddle down in the hole to sleep where no one could see me. The most difficult part had nothing to do with the car. It had everything to do with predators. You don't know fear until you've heard gravel crunching outside the windows at night. I parked behind the house of a longtime friend's mother. She was always drunk and knew what was going on out there in the garage and alley, but she never gave me any trouble.

By not showing up for my court appearance, things quickly went from very bad to a whole lot worse. I now had bail bondsman hunting me down, and for people like us who existed in the shadows trying to be as invisible as possible, my presence caused an uneasiness. No one wanted me around. Bail bondsmen will stop at nothing to recover a loss. They are ruthless and effective. Eventually, they caught up with my son's eighty-year-old great-grandmother and told her she would be subject to criminal prosecution for aiding and abetting if she did not reveal my whereabouts. I have no idea how anyone got that message through to me, but they did. I knew I had to turn myself in. I was out of options.

A crucial and critical moment happened in the parking lot when I arrived at the bail bondsman's office. There have been occasions in my life that I call "a moment of clarity," and this was certainly one of those times. It was a decision made in a split second that would have a monumental effect on the rest of my life. As I was walking from my vehicle to the door, I stopped, stepped back, and pulled out the bag of meth I had stuffed in my bra. I put it in the tie-down hole in the bed of the truck I was driving. That instant, that action kept me out of prison, and for that, I am eternally grateful.

The second I walked in the door, the bail bondsman arrested me, in the same manner, I had been arrested the last time: flat on the floor, arms handcuffed behind my back, foot on my head, and searched. While I was still going to jail, I would not go to prison for an additional drug charge. Although that moment of clarity wasn't one that would do me any spiritual good, it had changed my life forever.

The bail bondsman made sure he told me what a piece of crap he thought I was (that's the cleaned-up version). Of course, I agreed. He was just one more person in the long line of people who confirmed what I already believed about myself. He loaded me in the car and delivered me back to jail.

I did do one helpful thing while I was out on bail. I had bumped into a girl I had also seen in jail. I told her my status; I had jumped bail and couldn't turn in a clean urinalysis (UA), which the courts required. She suggested I go to the welfare office and tell them I was a drug addict. They would send me to a drug treatment center. Then, the judge would see I was changing, offer me mercy, and suspend the remainder of my jail sentence. I would be free to continue my lifestyle without any monitoring from the courts. That should work. The court system was requiring I change or do more jail time. Change or go to prison. I didn't know how to change and had no faith that I could.

At the welfare office, I unloaded my graphic story to a poor, unsuspecting employee. Graphic, ugly, and true. When I left that appointment, the woman did not doubt I was a drug addict. I told her every gory detail until she cut me off. My problem was the courts wanted me to provide regular urinalysis tests to check for drug use. There was no way in hell I could stop using. I needed that stuff like air to breathe. I qualified for the state's free drug treatment program and awaited a bed date, the date they would accept my arrival at the inpatient treatment center.

A Glimpse of Reality

"Self-loathing is another form of self-worship.
I need to be concerned when I'm the only thing on my mind."
—Heard in an AA meeting

I received my bed date for treatment while I was back in jail. My mom agreed to let me stay with her temporarily. I was driven to the Greyhound bus station by my probation officer, who bought me a ticket to Spokane. By this time, I'd had my day in court and been convicted of the felony. My probation officer allowed me to go to Spokane to stay with my mother until I entered the treatment center. He made sure I understood if I didn't show up, he was coming for me. I slept most of the time at my mother's house, not having slept more than sporadically for nearly five years. (Meth will do that to you, and the longer you're awake, the more you hallucinate.) I still couldn't see well, had never had a driver's license, and was a tenth-grade dropout. The future did not look bright, but then again, it never had.

In June of 1992, I got on another Greyhound bus that took me to the chemical dependency treatment center for my twenty-one-day turn at rehab, affectionately referred to as "spin-dry" by those exposed to addiction. When I arrived, I had no idea what to expect. I only knew this was supposed to keep me from going back to jail. I was there for all the wrong reasons, and yet God still used the situation for His glory. My selfish motives aside, thirty minutes after walking through the door, I met the first person who would give me hope.

I was a twenty-seven-year-old, foul-mouthed, street-hardened young woman. I was loud and abrasive, my face scarred from hard-living, legally blind, and scared to death. That fear manifested itself as anger. At my intake interview, I answered all the questions as clearly and concisely as I could. There were three components to this interview that impacted me:

1. My counselor said, "You seem to have an awful lot of pride, but I am not hearing a lot to be proud of." As cocky as I was, I was surprised that I accepted that from her, but I did. I only remember feeling my posture soften.

2. There were more questions, and then she asked, "Wow, aren't you tired? Living a life like that must take a lot of work." I had never thought about that before. I was tired. Big exhale. Tired. *Merriam-Webster's Collegiate Dictionary, 11th Edition* defines the word tired as an adjective meaning 1: drained of strength and energy: fatigued to the point of exhaustion 2: obviously worn down by hard use: run-down.

3. The finale was when she asked if I had ever considered suicide. I again answered honestly that no, I had not. She then turned in her chair to look at me and said compassionately yet sternly, "Really? Why not?" This silenced me. I don't know how long that silence lasted, but it offered me the clarity I needed. I had exhausted everything and everyone. I had nothing left. At that moment, I received the gift of desperation. If I were to survive, I would need to change. "Are you ready to try something different?" she asked. Yes, yes, I was.

This was my moment of clarity, and this was my place of hope. I wondered what would happen if I stopped trying to work the system and tried working the program?

My intake paperwork described my condition as "late-stage alcoholism," or what they commonly referred to as "body rot." I had abused myself, had allowed others to abuse me, and for years, I had deprived myself of food and sleep. My regular body functions were shutting down. Without the substances to prop me up, I was very, very tired.

Hope was something I'd never been offered before, at least not to my knowledge. There's a pretty good chance that the long line of well-meaning people who tried to help me along the way may have been offering me hope. I apparently needed to be desperate to want it. Desperation and a willingness to change would become the stepping-stones of my healing journey.

The counselor was also an alcoholic, but she had turned her life around. I couldn't wrap my mind around that, but I knew she understood the level of despair I'd experienced, which allowed me to hear her differently than I ever had heard anyone before. I would learn that approximately 80 percent of the staff there were recovering alcoholics and drug addicts. I came to believe I had been resistant to accepting help from people before because I didn't feel they could understand what I had felt and experienced. In his great wisdom, God put me in this place to be surrounded by people who knew exactly what it was like. It also meant they saw right through my BS. My pre-rehearsed victim routines were useless. You can't con a con.

The next twenty-one days were intense. I was encouraged not to dwell on my problems but rather to work on acceptance of my current reality—what a concept. We were required to attend three group therapy sessions a day, two lectures, and eat all our meals with our group. I complied with everything to the best of my ability, which wasn't much in those days. There wasn't much left of me, and I remember thinking that even all the other patients there were better off than I was. I had difficulty reading the material, but I made do. One of the receptionists brought me a magnifying glass. With that, I did the best

I could. I felt such an extreme sadness and loneliness over stepping away from everyone I knew in Tacoma. These were people I cared about and who were just a lot of fun, but I had to separate myself, not only geographically but completely. I came to believe what those who had been successful in their recovery told me. If I continued to put myself in positions (and that included mentally) of thinking fondly of the situations I had begged God to get me out of, I would find an opportunity to go back. They were right. My behavior would follow what my mind had decided. I'd seen it over and over again.

I was sad as I watched my fellow patients at the treatment center have guests visit and send flowers. As one person walked down the hall with flowers, her friend said to me, "Don't judge her because one of her clients sent her flowers." I already knew she was a prostitute, but I wasn't judging her. I was jealous that she had people who cared. It didn't matter who they were. I had no visitors while I was in treatment or jail until I was in family counseling, and even that was a struggle.

At the end of the program, I was moved to a different building for three days of programming with immediate family members since addiction surely affects the entire family. I had no one to participate. I asked my mother, and she said she could not take time off work. While there may have been some truth to that, we also both knew she did not want to discuss our family dynamic. Then or now. As a last resort, and at the encouragement of my counselor, I reached out to my son's paternal grandmother, the woman who now had custody of him. She told me she would make it, no matter what. When my mom found out, she suddenly was able to come. We went through this final phase of the program, carefully dodging the elephant in the room. Our problems ran deep, and we went to great lengths to try to keep our secrets hidden.

I was still required by the court to complete the rest of my sentence in the Pierce County Jail. After the program, I hopped on a Greyhound bus and went back to jail to do my time. This time I wasn't scared and wasn't going through withdrawal. I arrived with a very strong pair of reading glasses (a gift from my counselor) and *The Big Book of Alcoholics Anonymous*. I spent those thirty days looking forward to something for the first time in my life. This time I had an end date to my sentence. I kept to myself and read my book. I could not wait to have freedom. I had been oppressed and controlled for so long, and I was bursting at the seams. But it was an illusion that I would then be able to do whatever I wanted to do. There were authorities and rules to follow everywhere, and always would be.

When released from jail, I went to my mother's house in Spokane. She was between relationships and living alone. I did not give up the relationship with my co-defendant and boyfriend. Mark was in prison, and we had exchanged letters. When I went to live with my mother, I sent him her address and phone number. He called long-distance collect, and we would talk for hours. I look back now and think how thoughtless I was. I had no money, so my mother footed the bill for our phone calls.

Mark was attentive and complimentary, and I was still in deep need of love. It was the first time I'd ever heard kind things from a man who wasn't just saying them out of regret. I was lonely, scared, and felt deeply indebted to him for getting me out of that terrible relationship with Curtis. I felt such an intense obligation. I owed him, and I would spend a great deal of time trying to repay that debt (emphasis trying). We spent numerous hours on the phone to recant my daily trips to outpatient treatment and AA (Alcoholics Anonymous) meetings. He would tell me about the program he was attending and that he was also meeting with the prison chaplain. We talked about our future. We had been through so much together, and we both needed someone to trust. After a while, he was moved from medium security at the Washington State Penitentiary in Walla Walla, Washington, to Medical Lake Correctional Facility. Due to my exemplary adherence to my probation requirements and AA attendance, my probation officer wrote a letter of endorsement to the prison board.

I was allowed visitations with Mark, despite my felony conviction and the fact Mark was my co-defendant.

My probation required me to attend outpatient treatment. I would call in every morning and find out if I had a urinalysis test for that day. If I did, I had to show up and give a urine sample. I did everything they asked of me. I would have done more. The bus drivers were very helpful since I couldn't read the bus schedule or the street signs to the treatment center. The counselors treated me with respect. They suggested I attend women's meetings of AA, which I did. It was incredibly comforting to learn I was not alone. A bunch of people were out there just like me who had messed up their lives. Yet here they were, admitting all those disasters, and they were still able to smile, laugh, and hug one another.

Since my primary addiction had been drugs, not alcohol, I attended Narcotics Anonymous (NA) meetings first. I determined NA was not the best choice for me because I didn't encounter anyone with a solid clean time of more than two years at the meetings. I was looking for more than that, so I went to AA. The program recommends that you get a sponsor, and I was shopping for mine. I was looking for someone with some street smarts, some savvy, who might be fun to be around and had some "cool" factor. When it was suggested I ask someone to be a temporary sponsor, I mustered up the courage to ask a woman at my table. Only she didn't hear the word "temporary" and accepted the position.

I now know God didn't allow me to select my sponsor because I tended to revere my drug escapades as the glory days back in those early days. There is a phenomenon known as a "contact high." Remembering only the good stuff and sharing war stories was dangerous. God chose a sixty-plus-year-old woman with glasses that hung on a chain around her neck and smoked like a chimney. Her name was Joyce K., and she would lead me into a relationship with Jesus Christ. God would use this woman to save my life.

Chapter 6: Reaching Rock Bottom

What do you think the statement, "The worst day of my life and the best day of my life were the same day" means? Can you think of a devastating experience in your own life that turned out to be beneficial to you? Explain.

____

____

____

It wasn't until the third or fourth day of being in jail that I regained some mental clarity as the drugs slowly left my system. Have you ever tried to reason with someone under the influence? How did that go?

____

____

____

Reflect on *Webster's* definition of the word "tired" included in the text. Is there anything currently in your life that you are tired of? Explain.

____

____

____

The counselor at the treatment center was brutally honest and blunt. Why do you think she chose this method of communicating with me?

Would this communication style be the best choice for everyone?

No longer under the influence of any mind- or mood-altering substances, I could see the opportunity I was being offered. I refer to it as "the gift of desperation."

In what ways can desperation be a gift? How have you seen or experienced this? (Example: bravery, etc.)

As I emerged from treatment, I still felt indebted to Mark and a sense of obligation. He was also quick to remind me of all he had done for me, should I ever forget. Is there someone who mentions the favors they have done for you when they want something from you or when you step out on your own? How does this make you feel?

When this happens, can you identify the thought progression that draws you back into your previous role in that relationship?

I knew I needed a sponsor (mentor), but I wanted it to be on my terms. I had a specific type of person I wanted to act as a guide, but I found what I needed in Joyce K. In what ways have you decided you wanted help but put restrictions on exactly how and from where it would come? How did it turn out?

CHAPTER 7

Walking It Out

"Success leaves clues."

—Tony Robbins

JOYCE K. RECOMMENDED that I attend thirty meetings over thirty days, a very common suggestion sponsors make in the AA program. I didn't make it to all those meetings, but I sure made it to a lot of them. I was terrified, desperate, and willing to do whatever these people told me to do. They had come from a similar place of hopelessness and were now experiencing the vitality of life. Joyce K. and I worked diligently together. The importance of what I learned with her is why you'll find numerous AA one-liners and their philosophy throughout this book. I will always remember her telling me, "If it feels like you're coasting, you're going downhill." Those words would ring true over and over again. They are still true today.

Joyce's policy was that I call her every morning and check in, even if I just left a message. She made it clear she would not be calling me. If I truly wanted sobriety, I had to be the one to dial the phone. Several times she asked me what I had planned for the day, and I would say I had nothing planned. I was broke, blind, and didn't have a car. I mostly hung out in my bathrobe. She instructed me to set a time to rise every morning and take a shower and get dressed, whether I had somewhere to go or not. "Suit up and show up in your own life." She told me to act as if I had somewhere to be. Then I would be ready when the opportunity arose. I did this, and it was amazing what that one little step did for my self-esteem. I began to take walks around the block and do other small, healthy things because I was ready to face the day.

Joyce and I had a standing Sunday afternoon appointment where she would assign me homework out of *The Big Book of Alcoholics Anonymous*. While the book was not originally written as a textbook, we studied the disease of alcoholism and the patterns of behavior described by the program's forefathers. We looked for our own behavior patterns in their stories. I began to understand my condition was both mental and physical. I had a disease of the mind that manifested as an obsession for mind- and mood-altering substances. I had heard it said that addiction is the only disease that will convince you it is not trying to kill you. Cancer doesn't do that. I could see the evidence of physical craving. Once I ingested any mind or mood-altering substance, I experienced an overpowering physical urge for more, and no amount of logic could reason with it.

We spent numerous Sunday afternoons reviewing my work and my answers to how many times the word "control" or "attempted control" appeared in a chapter. We studied testimonies, written in 1939, of alcoholics who could not achieve control of their drinking "no matter how great the necessity or wish." I began to understand my attempts at the same were futile. Something amazing happened during this time; I lost my desire to drink and use drugs. They no longer dominated my thoughts. In these early days, I learned to trust Joyce. Once trust was established, I was able to begin to work on the Twelve Steps, which are suggested as a program of recovery. Although all of the Twelve Steps were important, a few were more significant in the step work I did with Joyce. I've highlighted these below.

(Note: "Alcoholics Anonymous is not allied with any sect,

denomination, politics, organization or institution; nor does it wish to engage in any controversy; neither endorses, nor opposes, any causes. Our primary purpose is to stay sober and help other alcoholics achieve sobriety." AA is not a "Christian" program. The experience Joyce K. and I had was solely our own.)

One Step at a Time

Step One: "We admitted we were powerless over alcohol, that our lives had become unmanageable."

I never had power over my consumption or my behavior once I indulged. In the presence of my trusted sponsor, I began to see and admit the overwhelming evidence. There was never enough, no matter what the substance. Once I had one drink, I had no logical thought of quitting, no matter what the intention was prior to that first drink. The craving and obsession overtook me. With alcohol, I blacked out much of the time. As my progression moved on to other substances, I could still identify an immediate lack of control at first use.

Step Two: "Came to believe that a Power greater than ourselves could restore us to sanity."

Since I qualified for many different Twelve-Step groups, I also attended Al-Anon, a support group for family members of alcoholics and addicts. They were a wonderful group of loving people learning to care for themselves. There were not many men in my area who attended, so I remember one gentleman well. He spoke wisely of the second step of Al-Anon, the "restoration of sanity." His story was like mine, mired in chaos, deception, and violence from his family of origin. When working with his sponsor, he became stuck on the second step (much like I did). He described being baffled by it and recriminating himself for not being able to progress through it. His breakthrough came when he understood that a restoration to sanity was not possible since he wasn't sure he'd ever glimpsed it. He needed instead to be introduced to sanity. He had no idea what it looked like in his life.

I had been accused regularly of being insane. But did I know anything else? Listening to that gentleman, I realized I would also need an introduction to sanity. While I never knew what his journey looked like after he admitted this perplexity, his sharing of it is forever etched in my mind. I am grateful because I saw myself in this camp. I couldn't be restored to what I never had.

I walked away from Al-Anon with a nugget of wisdom that day. I began to seek out people around me who stayed calm and did not overreact during disagreements. These people didn't pack a suitcase, declare the end of their relationship, and leave because of a heated discussion with their spouse. They stayed and persevered.

Did I believe there was a Power greater than myself? Absolutely, I believed that everyone, including God, was a power greater than myself. Did I believe He could restore me to sanity? That part took a little longer. Joyce worked with me as I tried to sort out my confusion. She asked, "Do you believe that God has the ability to restore you to sanity?" I answered, "Yes, I believe He is powerful enough." We could move on.

Step Three: "Made a decision to turn our will and our lives over to the care of God, as we understood Him."

There it was—the God thing again. Joyce had been a Catholic her entire life. My only experience with religion was the bitterness toward the Catholic Church that my mother so clearly displayed. The fear that good church people would come around and tell us how bad we were. I had always had an internal belief that God existed but was certain He had no interest, just disdain, for me. So here is where I got stuck. Who was this God, and where had He been all the times I needed help? I heard a variety of confusing things at meetings regarding the last part of this step, the "as we understood Him" part. Well, I had a belief in God. I believed He had better things to do than sit around being disappointed in me.

As time went on, I would hear about God being a loving Father, and my image of that was of a kindly old man in heaven who wanted nothing more than to hold me and tell me everything was going to be all right. That is where things came to a screeching halt. I met that notion with a hostile "no way." Are you kidding me? Every grown man I had ever been in a relationship with or witnessed being a parent was a louse. Some were even worse than a louse. I had been abandoned by my birth father and abused sexually and emotionally by my stepfather. So, who was this loving Father? I've seen kids dragged around through crack houses, drugged, beaten, and teased relentlessly by their parents, and I was a horrendous example of a parent myself. So, turning my will and my life over to another man, an invisible one? That wasn't going to happen.

Joyce never tried to convert me to any organized religion, but she asked if I was willing to believe. Over time, she broke down this step into bite-size pieces I could digest. I would hear ladies at meetings speak about the AA group being their Higher Power, and I would think that was weird. How could a group be your God? But they were sober, and I wanted to be, so who was I to judge?

Chapter 7: Walking It Out

As an AA sponsor, Joyce K. had a lot of hard-earned wisdom…and one-liners. What comes to mind when you think of these two things she told me early on in our relationship?

"If it feels like you're coasting, you're going downhill."
"Suit up and show up in your own life."

Why did Joyce delay me in starting the Twelve-Step program? What needed to be established *before* I could begin working the recovery program with her?

Have you ever moved into a new, intimate relationship (friendship or romantic) too quickly to have the information you shared used against you? What caused you to do this? How did it turn out?

I outline my personal experience with some of the Twelve Steps of Alcoholics Anonymous, which look different for everyone. Have you considered that each person has a unique experience working in the same program?

When someone fails at losing weight, we typically don't blame the diet but their lack of adherence to the program. Have you or someone you've known been unable to get clean/sober (or free of another hang-up) and blamed the recovery program? How has this chapter offered you a fresh perspective?

Step One: "We admitted we were powerless over alcohol—that our lives had become unmanageable."

Admitting powerlessness is counterintuitive to popular thinking, yet it is the first step to this recovery program. How do you think it creates a starting point?

If drugs or alcohol are not a problem for you, are there other things that can throw you off balance? Is there a person, place, or situation where you suddenly lose your resolve and become "powerless" when near them? Explain.

Step Two: "Came to believe that a Power greater than ourselves could restore us to sanity."

Webster's Dictionary defines sanity as "the condition of being sane. Sane: 1. Proceeding from a sound mind. 2. Mentally sound. 3. Able to anticipate and appraise the effect of one's actions." Describe a specific time when you were not "mentally sound" or weren't able to appraise the effect of your actions, if even for a moment.

Step Three: "Turned our will and our lives over to the care of God, as we understood Him."

I arrived at my early belief system by my mother's bitter outbursts regarding her church experiences and, later, by God's failure to live up to my expectations.

Take a moment to reflect on how you arrived at your belief system. Does it belong to you, or was it given to you? Explain.

The Work Continues

Step Four: "Made a searching and fearless moral inventory of ourselves."

I had no idea what this step even meant. After all, I felt better than I ever had. Joyce and the other ladies in my group were there to remind me that "We are not cured of alcoholism. What we have is a daily reprieve based on our spiritual condition." I was experiencing the benefits of AA, yes, but because we had studied the *Big Book* so much up to this point, I also knew the testimony of Bill W., one of the *Big Book*'s authors, that described the period prior to his relapse. He said, "All went well for a while, but I failed to enlarge my spiritual life." The peace I was experiencing could be lost, and I did not want that to happen. Again, fear was my motivation.

I can't remember how I began my personal inventory, but I had plenty of shame and regret that landed on those pages. Some of the biggest ones you know about: the inability to care for my child, the vindictive treatment of Curtis, and the abortions. These were the items that shouted the loudest. Joyce was a very patient woman. Week after week, we gently went deeper. One example was I had to admit I had driven the getaway car for burglaries and benefited from the spoils. I came face-to-face with the reality that I was no better than anyone else involved just because I hadn't broken the window and entered their home.

I could no longer hide behind the false pride that I was somehow better than the others when I had participated in the crime at any level. This was only one example of many other incidents and certainly wasn't the pinnacle of my madness. I could see I had made choices every step of the way. I was being introduced to the idea of personal responsibility, and it was humbling. Also on my list was all the money I had "borrowed" from people and never paid back, especially from those who had taken me in as a teenager. I began to understand why this step was important. Joyce would tell me that until I made peace with the fact that I had, in fact, participated in these activities, they remained negatively in my conscience, and they could diminish the work we were doing. She warned that they had the power to hold me back and would likely rear their ugly heads at the least opportune times. "You can deal with it, or you can revisit it," she noted. "The choice is yours."

So, I went on a list-making crusade. I wrote random things as they occurred to me. I began to see how the visions would pop up from my memories, seemingly unprompted and often, confirming what Joyce was telling me. They were cycling through me. I was amazed at how many "small" items repeated more frequently were burdens on my heart. I'd had enough of the program to know that our secrets keep us sick. I kept a tablet on the seat of my car, mostly writing in code so that if anyone saw my notes, they wouldn't be able to make any sense of them. This was the easy part.

Joyce and I discussed all my items, one by one, focusing on my role in each. I was surprised by how many excuses and justifications I had for the things I'd done. All the whys quickly came to the surface, often with much animation and defensiveness. Time after time, I focused on what someone else had done to put me in a situation where I then had limited options. I wanted out of any personal responsibility, and I was squirming and getting louder. I did not like getting backed into a corner! The difference in this situation from others I had experienced was that I wanted recovery. My pressure was coming from within and from someone I loved who loved me. It wasn't the hostile pressure from the streets. It was gentle, patient, and consistent.

I had spent my life up until that point effectively blaming people and situations for my actions and my shameful and regretful decisions. My sponsor, with her gravelly voice in that dark, smoke-filled apartment, just kept asking, "What was your role, Teresa? Which decisions were yours?" Finally, when I reached a point where I realized my justifications were futile, I sighed a slow exhale and slumped in my chair. I accepted my role. I lit another cigarette.

In most cases, I had made many small decisions along the way that had landed me in the "big" situation that was still haunting me, the one I had no way out of. I could see I was not always a victim, but a willing participant, perpetuating a cycle that had become normal and routine. Following each item, we discussed what the driving force behind each one might have been. Had I been lonely and just seeking acceptance and love? Was it pride, demanding to be noticed? Was it selfishness, taking my fair share while I had the opportunity? Who knows how long it took me to complete my personal inventory? It was months. Eventually, we moved on.

What do you think I mean when I write "Our secrets keep us sick?

____

____

____

In what harmful ways can emotional and spiritual weakness express itself? How have you experienced this in yourself and others?

____

____

____

Have you personally experienced being in a safe, gentle relationship where you were able to share your biggest regrets? What motivated you to want to share these?

____

____

____

Step Five: "Admitted to God, to ourselves, and to another human being the exact nature of our wrongs."

Joyce said one of our Sunday meetings would be devoted entirely to Step Five and to expect to be together for several hours. This step seemed redundant to me. I had already admitted these things to God, Joyce, and myself. Hadn't we all been in the room when we went through them? Whatever (eye-roll). We set a date.

We met on the living room floor of Joyce's apartment. I read each of my inventory items out loud and recited my role, leaving any mention of others' participation out of it. I read what need I was trying to fill from my decisions. Several times, Joyce asked me how the process of viewing these past experiences made me feel. I felt ashamed, guilty, and alone. I cried my way through that entire afternoon. The intensity of looking at my life in this condensed version was unprecedented. I had never experienced such honesty, and it was pouring out of me. I was shaking. Joyce held my hand from time to time as I wrenched from the pain I was releasing but rarely spoke. I told her I couldn't go on. It was too hard. She asked if it was harder than carrying this around with me every day. No. I continued. Somehow it felt like these things had been holding me up, and as I released them, my posture melted. I wept into the floor and lay there as I dropped the final sheet of paper. Silence. After a time, who knows how long, Joyce asked me two questions that altered my life forever.

Pointing to the wadded-up, tear-stained paper on the floor, she said, "This is what a life run on self-will looks like. Teresa, do you realize that this is the best you can do without God in your life?" I couldn't even speak. That pile of paper represented the results of my own freewill choices. I had to face that my selective memory had allowed me to believe that the insanity of my life was their fault, whoever "they" were in each scenario. I had believed I stood on higher ground because clearly, I was not a thief. I did not break into other people's homes and steal their belongings. I believed I had standards and had the ego to back that up. I was facing myself for the very first time and accepting that I did not have standards. When I condoned that behavior and participated in it at any level, a part of my soul died. In my spirit, I had felt conflicted, but I did it anyway. It was not my nature to do any of those things. So, every time it happened, I increased the hatred for the woman in the mirror. That pile of paper honestly represented the best I could do on my own, and I was deeply ashamed. Next, Joyce said, "This can change today if you would like it to. Would you like to accept Jesus as your Lord and Savior and leave these items with Him today?"

I recited the prayer of salvation that day and gave my shame to Him. I released my self-dependence, for the moment, and pondered that He had been waiting for me. I had a deep level of understanding that I had reached the absolute end of myself. I left Joyce's apartment that day broken and whole, spent and energized. I was acceptable to God, myself, and another human being, despite my shortcomings. Joyce asked me to spend the next couple of days quietly journaling my thoughts and feelings and not to make any major decisions. When I called her every morning, she would remind me to breathe.

Study Guide

The Girl in Your Wallet

Chapter 7: Walking It Out

Step Five: "Admitted to God, to ourselves, and to another human being the exact nature of our wrongs."

This step was monumental, but I cannot emphasize enough I was in the presence of a safe person. Up to this point, my "people-picker" had been underdeveloped. If you have shared your deepest secrets with the wrong people, I encourage you not to give up on people but to learn how to identify the right ones.

(For more on this, I suggest reading the book *Safe People: How to Find Relationships That Are Good for You* by Dr. Henry Cloud and Dr. John Townsend.)

In what ways have you been both the source and recipient of your pain and regret?

____

____

____

Joyce asked me two questions that altered my life forever:

- Did I see that my best efforts at running my own life had resulted in complete and utter ruin?
- Was I ready to accept Jesus as my Lord and Savior?

Accepting Jesus as my Lord and Savior would bring me out of a place of self-reliance (inevitable defeat for me) and into a God reliance. I entered a place of peace I didn't know was available to me.

Are you willing to make a similar decision? Are you at least willing to have an open mind? Why or why not?

___

___

___

Progress, not Perfection

Joyce had collected all those papers from my fifth step, and after I emerged from a time of quiet and reflection and could begin to hold my head up again, we used them.

Step Eight: "Made a list of all persons we had harmed and became willing to make amends to them all."

Hadn't I been through enough? I was angry, and I didn't mind showing it. I had done the work and faced the facts! Why now was I expected to air my dirty laundry in public? To me, this sounded like finding those who had already condemned me and giving them more fuel for their fires. Why confirm other people's low opinion of me? Was I seriously supposed to go back and make a spectacle of myself?

I did not want to do that. I was angry. I imagine I looked a bit like a three-year-old with my bottom lip out, arms crossed, kicking sand. Turns out anger is a great diversion from fear. This step also brought out quite a bit of foul language I hadn't used in a while. Joyce would listen to my extremes and then bring me back to center. She suggested I reread the step. There were two parts, and the first had been partially created by my fourth and fifth steps. "Teresa, can you make a list?" Yeah, whatever (eye-roll). We made a list. Willingness was now all that was required. Was I willing? Was I at least willing to become willing? Maybe we could start with some people who still chose to love me despite my abhorrent behavior. Maybe we could start with my family?

Joyce was working within guidelines developed and handed down to her through generations of sponsors in the program. All the tools were created and used by the ladies in this recovery circle, and they were healing. Not only did these women have substantial clean time, but they were also happy despite life's difficulties. I saw women become widows and grieve deeply without relapsing. I watched as they sat with one another, not speaking a word. I watched them deal with life on life's terms and repeat the slogan, "There is no situation so bad that a drink won't make it worse."

Although the grueling work on my fourth step had been a short time ago, I still had plenty of deeply embedded defense mechanisms to support my justifications. I'd think, "If they hadn't, I wouldn't have had to.... You don't know what they did!" It had been easier when I only had to confess to Joyce during the fifth step, but I had read the remaining steps, and I knew where we were headed. I was being prepared to face these people I had hurt, and I was becoming combative. How grateful I am for my beloved sponsor's patience, although I didn't recognize it at the time. It has taken years of reflection and the experience of writing this book to see in such a condensed version how loving this woman was. She never told me what to do, always listened, and responded gently.

Chapter 7: Walking It Out

Step Eight: "Made a list of all persons we have harmed and became willing to make amends to them all."

I made the switch from peace to anger in a split second. In what ways do you use anger to distract from fear?

Do you ever use anger to give you courage in difficult situations?

I quote the AA slogan, "There is no situation so bad that a drink won't make it worse."

What substance or behavior would you use to fill in the blank?

"There is no situation so bad, that ________________ won't make it worse." (Example: going back to an ex, food, etc.)

Step Nine: "Made direct amends to such people wherever possible, except when to do so would injure them or others."

Joyce gave me the assignment to write letters to the people I'd hurt. So, I wrote. I brought the letters to our Sunday afternoon meetings and read them aloud to Joyce. They all started the same way.

> "Dear ________, As part of my recovery program, I am making amends to people I have harmed. I want you to know I recognize and regret doing ________, which caused you harm. I was selfish and thoughtless, and I am sorry for my actions."

Then, just as we had done before, we edited out all of my blaming and justifications, and to make amends, I met with some people face-to-face. Some received my letter by mail. Some of the letters I simply read aloud to my sponsor because they fell into the last category of having the potential of "injuring another person." This included, but was not limited to, people who had left those old lives behind and for whom bringing up the past was counterproductive. This last category also included people with whom I had a deep-seated desire just to see again and wanted to use this step as an excuse to make contact. Joyce was nobody's fool and was happy to continue to ask me what the driving force was until I recognized my selfish motives.

One major regret I have is not including myself as someone I had harmed. I wish I had written a letter to myself. In hindsight, I can see I had been both the source and recipient of much pain and regret. It is exhausting to hold a grudge against yourself, yet I have. It has cycled around in my conscience for decades, serving no good purpose. I have no illusion that I would have written and read a letter to myself and it would have been a relationship immediately restored. Still, it may have been helpful to implement the process of healing earlier. My relationship with myself has been the most difficult one for me to reconcile.

Step Twelve: "Having had a spiritual awakening as a result of these steps, we tried to carry this message to alcoholics and to practice these principles in all our affairs."

Joyce wanted me to pass along to others what had been given to me. She wanted me to sponsor other women and participate more fully in meetings. Whenever I would tell her I didn't have time to go to more meetings, she would tell me if I went to more meetings, I would have more time. She was right. When I got my mind and spirit in balance and my focus on others, the rest of the time was more productive. I struggled less, but I was selfish and was out to get what I needed. I told her I would think about it, but I didn't. I grew defiant as my attention turned to living out all the dreams Mark and I had discussed in those endless phone calls from prison, including becoming his wife. I slowly created distance between Joyce and myself.

Step Nine: "Made direct amends to such people wherever possible, except when to do so would injure them or others."

This step suggests we think through our actions' possible outcomes, even when our motives are good. Joyce taught me to "play that movie through to the end" before taking action or having difficult conversations (a concept I am still working on).

How have your attempts to "clear the air" or perhaps ease your conscience inadvertently harmed another person? Explain.

What is the relationship between vulnerability and courage? How do you resolve the thinking that being vulnerable gives other people the tools to hurt you?

Step Twelve: "Having had a spiritual awakening as the result of these Steps, we tried to carry this message to alcoholics and to practice these principles in all our affairs."

I achieved sobriety but failed to understand and adhere to the maintenance portion of the program. In what areas have you achieved success only to backslide due to abandoning the actions it took to reach it?

CHAPTER 8

Binding with Brokenness

"The greatest threat that I need to be rescued from is myself. Everything comes a lot easier after that."
—Craig D. Lounsbrough

THE LAST TIME I saw Joyce was at a large breakfast meeting in a restaurant on a Sunday morning. She introduced herself, spoke, and then called on me to speak next. I introduced myself, declined to talk, and did not stay in close contact with her. This stands as one of my biggest regrets. I was incredibly selfish and shortsighted. I justified my lack of helping others by ruminating mantras in my head about how busy and unqualified I was. I was now preparing to be a supporting wife! I can barely put these words on paper for the ridiculousness of them. I had yet to uncover just how deeply the training was implanted in me that the man comes first.

When I was seventeen and had married Curtis, he said he would take care of me. Of course, I knew this was exactly what I needed. Curtis would "save me" from my family of origin. I also mentioned I was still technically married to Curtis when I met Mark. Sound familiar? He would "save" me from Curtis.

At this juncture in my life, my phone conversations with Mark began to focus on marriage. Neither of us had ever been able to trust someone else, so since we were still together after everything we'd been through, we decided we could trust each other. Marrying Mark was not only discouraged by the ladies I was meeting with at Alcoholics Anonymous but also by my family and even the probation officer who wrote the very letter that got me into prison. Despite all their counsel, I was determined. He did not hit me, knew my past, accepted it, and was better than any man I had observed before.

We attended premarital counseling with the prison chaplain, which amounted to a couple of conversations about the biblical view of marriage. I am sure the chaplain felt like he had imparted wisdom to us, but I wasn't listening. I had the goal in mind. In March of 1993, we were married in the prison chapel. I went to my second wedding after having my bag searched and walking through a metal detector. My mother and Mark's cellmate served as witnesses.

Inmates Make Great Boyfriends

Mark had other people's girlfriends drive me to the prison to see him. I visited every week. He sent letters in envelopes adorned with artwork for which he had traded his commissary items. There were poems of sweetness about what our lives would be like in the future, with my name slipped in to make it personalized. The two of us had stuck together through all of this. What could possibly tear us apart? For Christmas, I received a necklace and earring set that he had made in the shop at the prison.

When the public asks why in the world would women want to date a man who's in prison, I usually just smile inwardly and let them speculate. I have firsthand experience: inmates make excellent boyfriends. They always call when they say they will and they are happy to see you on visiting day. They are full of compliments about how wonderful and beautiful you are, and then there are the gifts. How sweet that even on the inside, he would be able to give me earrings!

He was likely trading the money given to him on his account for jewelry that some other guy made in the workshop.

What the other girls and I didn't know at the time is that we all got the same poem and the same envelopes that made us dreamy. One guy is the artist and draws beautiful scenes on the envelopes. Another writes poetry about a future of love and companionship and slips in our names to personalize it. They exchange goods and services with each other to keep their girlfriends on the hook. It is part of a long-standing system that works. Excellent boyfriends are always there when they're supposed to be and long to hear from you. You have their undivided attention because they have nothing else to do. They're full of gifts and praise. Beware because the attention and adoration can change dramatically when they get out and have many other options. I speak the truth.

The flip side is also true. You can keep up the illusion by hiding your flaws and shortcomings on visiting day. You can leave a little spending money on their books (credit accounts), accept the phone charges, and stop by on the weekend for a bit of hand holding while you dream of a happy future together. If you have had a happy ending in this scenario, good for you. I did not. I was living in a fantasy that could not hold up in the real world.

Nothing New Under the Sun

Many years later, I agreed to visit an old friend in prison. As I walked on the sidewalk between fences wrapped in barbed wire, I heard a male voice say, "Hey, is that Teresa?" I had no idea who it was, but it surprised me that after so many years, someone still recognized me. I kept walking. I went in, showed my ID, passed through security, and seated myself at the assigned table. Tim came in with the rest of the guys and gave me a big, allowable hug. While we were visiting, he kept looking over my shoulder at someone. He said, "You don't recognize him, do you? That's Hanson over there."

Hanson had been in and out of prison since the 1980s when we ran in the same circles. When I turned around to look, he was on his way over to our table. He reached out for a hug, which was not allowed because I was not his authorized visitor. As the guard yelled at him, I asked if he would be in trouble for the hug. He replied, "Totally worth it." I asked if this was going to be his last stay. He smiled wryly and said, "We'll see." It seemed he had made peace with this way of life. It happens.

As Hanson returned to his table, I saw his visitor was a woman who looked much like how I described my sponsor, wearing a gold chain on her glasses. She was very put together but super-conservative in her flowery top and neat slacks. She was also much, much older than him. I asked, "Is that his girlfriend?" I was told, "That's his Saturday girlfriend. There's someone different here on Sundays."

Ladies, be very careful not to gauge the quality of your relationship with a guy when one of you is incarcerated. You could be in for a big disappointment because all that loving, single-minded attention may very well change when he gets out. I will pass on to you the same suggestion my sponsor gave me: see how things go on the outside for a year before you get married. It was sound advice. I sure wish I had listened.

When people who have stuck by you through thick and thin are concerned about the new person in your life, consider their input. At the very least, be cautious. Don't do what I did and tell your new friend how they can hurt you and, therefore, manipulate you. Remember, trust takes time.

Mark and I were now legally married. As such, we could get on the waiting list for conjugal or "trailer visits." These are days spent in a mobile home on the prison grounds, designed to help preserve the marital relationship. I learned two things in that trailer. One was that without the influence of drugs, we were awkward and self-conscious being intimate. The second I chose to ignore but shouldn't have. He asked me to sneak in contraband. I don't remember what exactly he wanted, but it wasn't drugs or anything "that serious," according to him. I just remember the pressure. I was trying to live an honest life and was having enough trouble with my own voices trying to get me to compromise. Now I had his voice opposing my newly awakened conscience as well. Both the lack of chemistry from being intimate and the pressure to get his way would last our entire relationship.

Accepting Help

I have been a grateful recipient of many publicly funded programs. The inpatient and outpatient treatment centers were paid in full by the Department of Social and Health Services (DSHS). Further, the medical coverage I received allowed me the much-needed eye surgery that restored vision in my damaged eye. I was also given aid by the Department of Vocational Rehabilitation (DVR) in a $300 clothing voucher at Kmart. I cannot even tell you how excited and confused I was that day! To the best of my knowledge, I never had selected my own pieces of clothing in my life. That is unless you included the shadier, illegal methods I'd used. Before that, everything I had received had been by donation through a group home and a uniform provided for me through Job Corps or birthday and Christmas gifts bought by someone else. I walked through Kmart with a calculator in hand and spent hours in the dressing room carefully selecting each item. I was filled with happiness but also unsure of how to dress. Who was I becoming?

I attended a publicly funded program called Project Self-Sufficiency at the local community college. Twenty women were in the class. Most were single moms participating in a welfare-to-work program. I was the only one in the room who didn't have my child at home. It became very difficult for me to explain, in the context of casual conversation, why my son did not live with me. I made multiple attempts to answer this question as quickly and easily as possible and then shift the conversation to a different topic. (If this is your situation, I would suggest using a simple, honest answer to avoid the panic of this happening. The fear of being asked this question was crippling.)

Project Self-Sufficiency had speakers from various businesses come in and talk to us about entering the workforce. Having no high school diploma and no work experience outside of working at the state fair, I heard a lot of useful information. We learned how to conduct ourselves in a job interview, how important first impressions and body language were, and basic keyboarding and calculator skills. We had an independent sales consultant from Jafra Cosmetics teach us how to wear makeup appropriately. This part was especially important to me because I had always been heavy-handed with makeup, looking like I was going to a nightclub instead of work.

Dealing with Doubt

Life lesson: Don't believe everything you think.

I began again to attend the AA program, although I never participated fully in the group environment. I found it difficult to talk to people and left as soon as the meeting was over, not taking any time to socialize. I constantly berated myself. I would rehearse over and over in my head some stupid thing I shouldn't have said. Constant self-criticism prevented me from growing and accepting myself. I was locked in that cycle for a very long time; it still crops up to this day. Long after my abusers were gone, I carried their voices in my head, reminding me at every turn of who I was and who I wasn't. I believed it was just a matter of time before I'd be discovered as a fraud with every level of success I achieved. Yet I endured. I had regularly scheduled meetings with my probation officer where we would review the criteria outlined by the court. I was an exemplary participant and was very motivated to escape my previous life. I was scared, for sure, but driven because of it.

I felt very awkward interacting with other people. If I had ever had social skills, which is questionable, they had been lost on the streets. It was common for people to say to me, "Wow, that was pretty harsh, wasn't it?" "You're just mean," or "There are nicer ways to say things, you know." I was trying, and I thought I was being gentle. Manners were not something taught to me as a child. Later, I would learn that wasn't entirely the problem. Having been silenced and invisible for so many years, I had many opinions bursting out of me. While being opinionated isn't all that uncommon, it took a while to learn that the problem was the hostility that accompanied my opinions. It prevented others from receiving information when presented with so much forcefulness. Now that I was no longer silenced, I had swung too far the other way. With a little more maturity, I learned to communicate more effectively, and I realized that sometimes I didn't need to share my opinion at all.

Finding Success

In 1992, I applied for a grant to attend Spokane Community College to study commercial baking. I never missed a day of school. I absolutely loved it. My schooling led to working part-time at a little muffin shop by our house. Being as blunt and direct as I was, I typically got along better with men than women. I could say what I meant with men, and they'd accept it, and we'd be done. There seemed to be some sort of mysterious protocol or formula with women, and I didn't know the code. I wanted to do the best I could, but the environment at this job was not conducive to that goal. My coworkers, all women, were gossips, backstabbers, and phony. We all had different days off, and whoever was off that day was whom they talked about during lunch. Still, working there became one of the best learning experiences of my life. Honestly, I learned that I never wanted to experience anything like that ever again. I would remember this later when I came into a position where I made the rules.

Study Guide

The Girl in Your Wallet

Chapter 8: Binding with Brokenness

Mark "knew my past, accepted it...." I based a life-changing decision on my core desire to be seen, known, and understood. How can you relate?

In what ways do "inmates make great boyfriends"? How did this perspective surprise you?

Despite my sponsor's thoughts, my group's input, and my probation officer's counsel, my second wedding took place in the prison chapel. Take a moment to reflect on your suggestions and advice to others. How much control do we really have over another's person's decisions?

____

____

____

On the outside, I looked determined and was moving forward. What was my self-talk like?

____

____

____

What does your inner voice say? Is there a repeating mantra about your "true identity"?

____

____

____

CHAPTER 9

Stepping in the Right Direction

"He that is faithful in a very little is faithful also in much: and he that is unrighteous in a very little is unrighteous also in much."
— Luke 16:10 (ASV)

IN JUNE OF 1994, during the last quarter of my schooling, I walked into Coeur d'Alene French Baking Company wearing my bakers' whites from my community college classes. My instructor had coached me that I should expect an entry-level wage of $6.00 per hour because of my lack of experience. I filled out my one-page application and spent five minutes talking with the owner. I walked out with a job making $5.00 per hour, minimum wage at the time, and with a promised performance review in thirty days. I would also receive credit for school while I was working in my industry.

I'm not sure why, but my supervisor, Scotty, always had me arrive two hours before the rest of the crew so I could work directly with him. I suspect it was because he knew I had ambition in the field. Being a small, family-owned company, the wages were low, and no one came in with experience. We worked in the production department, which meant we dealt with all the raw ingredients and scaled, mixed, and formed the dough into dinner rolls, hamburger buns, and loaves. In the beginning, I mostly counted and oiled baking pans until the other four crew members arrived. I discovered I was fascinated by manufacturing and watching how all the forming machines worked. It was so clever. I have always loved creative problem-solving.

Scotty took the time to give me an overview of the entire operation. He introduced me to the oven operators, packing crews, and office staff. At the end of every shift, we walked together through the racks of baked bread. I learned to identify the finished products. We discussed tray placement accuracy and did bread tastings. While he likely felt he was being polite and courteous, he made me feel like a valued member of the team. At that time, I was still very reserved, trying to hold down my job while still going to school twenty-five hours a week. I was terrified of "being found out." I knew if anyone asked me about my background, I would need to be honest. I had committed to a lifestyle that demanded rigorous honesty, and I would do my best. However, that decision did not relieve me of the anxiety of fearing that someone would see through me one day. I was also still operating in my well-established pattern of anxiety. I was guarded.

Surviving Setbacks

Then one Friday, when I picked up my paycheck, I noticed a huge error on it. I had only recently begun to make enough money to clear about $500 every two weeks, and this check was for just under $300! I examined the stub and saw a deduction for a garnishment. I went back in to discuss the error with the woman in Human Resources. She produced documents from the courts showing past-due child support in excess of $10,000! They would be deducting 50 percent of my paychecks well into the future.

I spiraled out of control. All those old thought-patterns reared their ugly head: Just when I try to turn things around, why me? Why me? Poor me! My thoughts were a paranoid frenzy: How would we survive? Call your sponsor! Why? She doesn't have any money! Call your mom and ask her for money! Sell this car. You should never have bought it! The committee in my head argued nonstop for days. I went to work in a fog, wondering why I was going to work at all. I was on autopilot. Then the letter came in the mail.

My ex-mother-in-law and child's legal guardian sent me a card with a letter in it. She told me how happy she was that I was cleaned up and doing well and that she had contacted DSHS (Department of Social and Health Services) and given them my current contact information. She felt I was doing well enough to begin to pay restitution for my previous life choices.

I was overcome with emotions. On the one hand, I agreed with her. I did owe a debt of gratitude to those who had helped this young child I had brought into the world. On the other hand, I was enraged. How dare she! Who was she to determine when I was doing "well enough"? I barely had my head above water and had only recently moved out of my mother's basement. Mark and I lived in a 600-square-foot home. She signed the letter with "I love you, Honey." I thought, *What a crock! Someone who loved me would have asked how I was doing and worked with me on a plan.*

Mark felt very strongly about this too and made no small ruckus about how this wasn't his obligation. It was my past, and Christopher was not his kid. He felt his standard of living should not be affected by my past decisions. He eventually accepted that this was our reality together since we were married, but he grumbled on an ongoing basis for years.

I drove down to the DSHS office to plead my case. Surely, they would be reasonable. I was trying to turn my life around. I was also barely making more than minimum wage. During a good portion of the ride there, I fumbled madly in my purse, digging for something I simply could not find. Finally, it occurred to me I was looking for my cigarettes. I had been a nonsmoker for a couple of months, and this was the first big stress trigger. Boy, did I want that cigarette! No,

I needed that cigarette, and there were none to be found.

When I got to the DSHS office, I walked up to the counter, took my number, and sat down. I had been rehearsing my story for days. I practiced with Mark. After all, I was an expert in making people feel sorry for me; I had been doing it for years. When my number was called, the woman at the counter cut me off in midsentence. She told me she had no authority to change any part of the order. Because the courts had ordered it, it could only be undone by the courts. I needed a lawyer.

Eventually, I had the payment reduced to a reasonable amount, and life carried on. I found that I did not have to drink, smoke, or use drugs during or because of this crisis. The tension in my marriage remained, however.

Study Guide

The Girl in Your Wallet

Chapter 9: Stepping in the Right Direction

A financial crisis is one of the most stressful life events. What did I learn as I navigated the wage garnishment for back child support?

____

____

____

Are you able to review difficult situations for lessons without a critical voice?

____

____

____

CHAPTER 10

Learning to Play Well With Others

"All things are difficult before they are easy."

—Thomas Fuller

AS I BEGAN to understand what was expected of me in my job and became more comfortable with Scotty, I learned how to use scales differently from those used at the college. Scotty explained the importance of order when mixing dough. (Yeast and salt do not play well in the staging process.) I made mistakes, had successes, and began to develop confidence.

I soon moved from prepping bread pans to following recipes and mixing the various doughs. When the night shift supervisor quit, Scotty took his place. He told the owner I should be the one to run the a.m. shift. At first, I protested, feeling unqualified. I wanted the challenge of running my own shift, but I was terrified of the responsibility. Taking it on would make my nervousness even worse. There were others on our team, specifically one who had been there longer than I had, who felt the position should be theirs.

My coworker Norman was very vocal from the start about how he felt about me as a person, a woman, and an inferior employee. As coworkers, we hadn't been friends, but now that I would have the authority to tell him what to do, he was having none of it. If I asked him to do anything, he flat out told me to screw myself. "F—k you" and "No chick is going to tell me what to do" would spew from his mouth. While he said it quietly enough so only our crew could hear him, it still rattled me. As he heckled my work, I made major scaling mistakes. I had to throw out batches of bread dough. Scotty was supporting me from the nightshift, and the rest of the team did Norman's work while he griped and moaned. But none of us stood up to him. It took everything I had not to release a barrage of profanity on this guy. I was well-armed and could have sliced right into him with ease with my words. He thought he was tough, but I had survived far worse men than him. However, my dilemma was I needed this job on my resume alongside my formal training, and when I decided it was time to go, I was going to need a letter of recommendation. Norman played no role in my endgame and was merely a speed bump and test of my endurance. I kept my eyes focused on the prize. Nothing was going to divert me from my goal. I was determined never to return to where I'd come from, and there was no turning back. I suffered, was stressed, and lost sleep. But I waited him out. As a team, we ignored him. Eventually, his lack of ambition, constant complaining, and poor attendance would be his undoing.

Looking back, I'm very grateful for that experience with Norman. I learned to deal with a difficult situation without violence or profanity, although at the time, avoidance was all I was capable of. As it is with using any new muscle, I had been shaky and unstable, but I'd begun to flex it. I also learned how not to attack. Maturing has taught me to confront situations and resolve conflicts. Back then, I didn't know this option. I knew either to take him down or stay away. What gave me the restraint to walk away was the knowledge that the life I'd known before was lying in wait for me. My drive forward was to never, ever go back there. Even now, no matter how far away from it I get, that past life is still there, just a drink away. Or, in this case, it might be only a confrontation away.

I can pull up that pain of devastation, hopelessness, and hating myself in a second. Avoidance was my first defense, and I took baby steps from there. I learned a great deal about the quality of a work environment where everyone is valued. I also learned to deal with difficult situations without violence or profanity. But I've never lost the memory of how much I despised working with a bully. Once I had the authority to make sure it didn't happen again, I carried that knowledge into ownership, and fairness and respect became company core values.

Soon after Norman left, I saw a new face across the room. Carl had been hired as the packing supervisor, but I had not been introduced to him. Shortly after his hire, I began noticing people were acting differently around me. I learned Carl was a gossip and a troublemaker and had included me in his stories. My reaction this time was completely different from what it had been with Norman. I took Carl head-on. He told me he thought I was an idiot, like everyone else, and he was just having a little fun. I should lighten up. I told him firmly, "You thought wrong. Keep me out of your conversations, or you are going to have a much bigger problem." I may have come on too strong or used some bad language. But, working on my new confidence muscle, I was getting stronger.

Scotty stayed on the night shift and the morning shift became mine. Every morning, Bob, the owner, would do a walk-through and check in with me. I saw it mostly as pleasantries, but his recognition mattered to me. Our crew had become very good at using the production equipment, procedures, and flow as we had been instructed, and there were lots of opportunities for improvement. One day I tried a new way of processing bread that would go faster and free up baking trays and racks to move them back into the rotation sooner. When I saw how well it worked, I managed to find the courage to approach Bob before the rest of the office staff arrived. As I placed the two different pieces of bread on his desk, he told me how good they looked and praised me for the results. When I nervously explained that I had produced them two different ways, one at a significant savings of labor, I gained his full attention. He even went so far as to walk out to the production floor so I could demonstrate the difference between the current way bread was being produced and my improved process. He asked me to do it again the next day, and we'd look at the results.

I was just trying to be helpful, and I was successful at it. What I didn't realize at the time was my gift for process improvement and problem-solving. I was only beginning to tap into this talent, but I had a keen eye for it and the knowledge that to a small business, pennies matter. Here is where my business relationship with Bob began to change.

I continued to present my process improvement ideas and suggestions, and they were well received by management but not so much by the other production crews. My team was outproducing them, and there was pressure for them to keep up. I was not popular with the hourly employees, which was understandable. I was, however, becoming very good at my job, earning more money, and redefining the position as I went. I had been unpopular before. I could deal with this.

In 1996, Bob approached me about a new bakery they were planning to open in the Seattle area. Knowing I had spent many years on that side of the state, Bob wondered if I would be interested in relocating. I was much more comfortable talking with him by then, and he trusted me enough to allow me to streamline production as I saw fit, even asking me to consult on equipment purchases on occasion. I saw it as an opportunity to move closer to my son. So, Mark and I agreed to move to the Seattle area. Though the company paid no relocation expenses, I was getting something I desperately wanted. We loaded up a truck that was bigger than our house and drove across the Cascade Mountains.

In early 1997, Bob had signed a lease for a 12,000 square-foot facility located in the country's fourth-largest manufacturing district. I

went from working a 4:00 a.m. shift on a quiet back road in Spokane to starting up a twenty-four-hour operation in the center of a large industrial park. Things were moving at lightning speed. I had no idea what I had signed up for. If I had known, I might have run screaming in the other direction. I had assumed Bob had a plan. I was about to learn he had a plan for me to work it all out, and I did the hard way.

Bob would spend two days a week at my location. My area had a much higher cost of living, and we were hiring at minimum wage with no benefits. Bob seemed to believe I could talk good workers into taking less money. I could not. When I conveyed my frustration and difficulties to him, he'd tell me I would figure it out. Looking back, I apparently did, but I have no idea how I managed it. Most of the people interested in these jobs came from immigration assistance organizations. It would be their first job in the United States, and almost all of them had little English-speaking skills. Hiring became an exercise in logistics. It became more about getting warm bodies into all the time slots rather than building a team. When interviewing for jobs, they brought interpreters. However, once they came to work their shift, they didn't have interpreters, so I had very little ability to communicate with them. We accomplished tasks through a lot of "show-and-tell" rather than actual job training. What made matters even worse was that they also couldn't communicate with each other. We had Ukrainians, Kurds, Ethiopians, Bosnians, and others working together. They were wonderful people and eager to work, but we had a big communication problem.

When we started production, a few people from the Spokane bakery came to help train new employees. Again, we were a twenty-four-hour operation with a perishable product. It's all a blur now, and I don't remember getting any sleep. I was at the bakery, thinking about the bakery or talking to someone on the phone about the bakery. This went on for years and became my sense of self-worth. The job was my life. I couldn't risk failure.

Although we threw many, many products away in those early days, eventually, we found a rhythm. A few key people were given shifts to run, but the language barrier was always a struggle. Employee turnover was high. We were the first job for many new immigrants in the country. They stayed for about three months, ostensibly long enough to understand the bus systems and work ethic and find permanent housing. Then they moved on to jobs that paid more and had benefits. It was a frustrating cycle that repeated itself over and over. We could have retained some of them by paying a higher wage, but I did not have the authority to grant them more money.

In providing detail about those early years, I intend to show how I learned to develop endurance and social skills through the experience. I won't minimize that I made huge mistakes along the way. I addressed issues about personal hygiene that went terribly wrong. I mediated arguments between employees that were based on cultural differences I knew nothing about. Being female, dealing with some of these ethnicities was always an issue. There was a tremendous amount of personal drama. I just wanted to get bread baked and out the door successfully. Employees walked out on me, a few calling me names as they passed, slamming the door behind them.

At the same time, I was the point of contact for every construction contractor coming in to get the facility up and running and in an operating condition that was up to code. I knew how to make bread, schedule shifts, and motivate people. I knew nothing about plumbing, electrical, or food safety inspections. Contractors would show up and expect me to know why they were there and what I needed from them. I did not. So I fumbled my way through it all, running on pure tenacity. My drive and endurance were based on not failing rather than succeeding. I was never headed toward something but running instead from something else.

I had less trouble with the contractors because they were mostly men and my direct, rough-around-the-edges communication style was more appropriate with them. I didn't take any crap from them and had no problem standing up to those who talked down to me. Due to all of these experiences, I settled into a more confident sense of self. For the first time, I was learning who I was, although, at the time, I couldn't see it. Eventually, my brash exterior became one of confidence rather than confrontation. Personal confidence would come much later.

In time, Bob sold the Spokane bakery and moved to Seattle. He and I would work in closer proximity to each other, three to four days per week. He began to trust me more and more, leaving me several blank, signed checks for any needs I might have in his absence. Initially, I had to call and get permission to write a check. After a while, I became a signer on the accounts. I had purchasing authority with our vendor accounts and handled payroll, including my own. Looking back now, it seems he may have been testing me. He made certain I knew he was tracking the bank accounts, asking me random questions about things I had purchased and not really paying attention to my answers. I made mistakes and disappointed him occasionally, and then he'd let me know what he would have preferred I'd done. I listened and learned from it. I did not want to disappoint him.

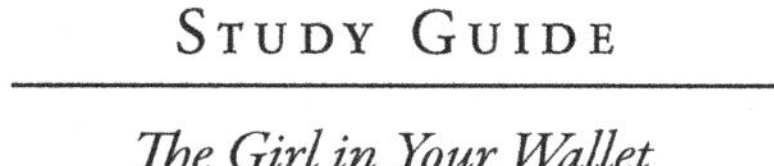

Study Guide

The Girl in Your Wallet

Chapter 10: Learning to Play Well With Others

Have you ever had a "Norman" in your life? If so, how did you respond, and what were the results? Were you then, or are you now able to consider it an opportunity for growth?

Does the memory still invoke powerful emotions? Are they helpful, or do you experience the anger/frustration all over again when you reflect on it?

Making mistakes is a vital part of learning and growing. How can you change your inner dialogue to incorporate the idea of "using a new muscle"?

Why was I becoming more and more unpopular with my coworkers?

Have you abandoned a course of action for acceptance? If so, how did you feel about yourself afterward?

CHAPTER 11

Mistaking Motives

"You will continue to suffer if you have an emotional reaction to everything that is said to you... true power is restraint. If words control you, that means everyone else can control you. Breathe and allow things to pass."

—Warren Buffet

AS GENEROUS AS Bob was in allowing me to grow my skills and provide me with opportunities, there were times I disagreed with him. My spiritual growth as a Christian and my AA program required effort and sincere honesty in all my dealings. I was encouraged on more than one occasion to turn a blind eye to some office activities. Occasionally, it was my job to write letters, which he would edit. One day, I refused to sign one of them. In essence, I told him, "I write these for you because it's my job, but I am not going to sign this as it is written." Taking this stance was a very scary place for me to be. I had a lot to lose. He gave me an abrupt, "Okay," and I went back into my office.

Soon after, when we discussed an issue, he seemed to imply I wasn't completely honest with him. My response was, "I don't know why you feel that way. I have always done my best to be honest with you. I am the one who brings you good news, bad news, and potential solutions to problems. If I were being dishonest, I don't think it would make sense for me to do that."

These two incidents preceded a very difficult time for us. Bob began leaving for days, sometimes weeks at a time, which wasn't so difficult since he wasn't involved in daily operations. Though when questions or problems would arise, and I needed guidance, he was slow to return my calls and was short with me on the phone. I was frustrated by his rejection and withdrew from him. After about four months of his detachment, I began looking for another job. I only wish I had prayed about this course of action first.

I applied for a position with a muffin and pastry bakery up the road about a mile. I dropped off my resume, and they lost it. I mailed another, and they said they didn't get it. Then I asked if I could schedule an interview and bring another copy of my resume with me. They said yes, but the interview was not a stellar experience for them or me. It was awkward, to say the least. During the interview, the owner left the decision up to the production manager and then abruptly left the room. Even though the pay was less than I'd wanted, he offered me the position, and I accepted. I gave Bob my two-week notice, and he received it with a short, "Okay then." I spent the next two weeks acting like a wild woman, trying to prepare Rika, the production manager, to take on additional tasks. I prepared lists, purchasing calendars, and payroll instructions. I did everything I could think of to take care of them, but two weeks was not much time to accomplish everything that needed to be done.

I started work at the new bakery on a Monday morning and knew I'd made a big mistake within an hour. The effort and frustration I'd experienced trying to get an interview with the company should have been my first clue that they weren't all that impressed with me in the first place. My second clue was that I wasn't impressed with them either. Could they really be that disorganized and crass? Yes, so it seemed. I had not asked God for direction but had followed earthly wisdom of "follow-up and be persistent." I was reeling from Bob's rejection, and I had made an emotional decision with my career. I had come from a history of painful rejection, and to protect myself, I'd retreated. I cared for Bob like a father, although he didn't know that. I had never experienced paternal love, and his approval of me drove my hard work. When he withdrew, so did I.

Within that first hour on the job, I learned that my new work environment included blatant profanity. Many of my coworkers smoked, which was still a great temptation for me. As I passed through the facility, I heard people telling dirty jokes out in the open. It appeared as though I had walked into a business with values that conflicted greatly from mine. I went home that night exhausted and discouraged but resolved that I had made the decision and would have to live with it.

Tuesday morning at 3:00 a.m. I was getting ready for work. As I bent over, I suddenly felt something odd and lumpy in my right eye. I blinked a few times, but my eye still felt strange. I looked at the items on the shelf and noticed everything was blurry. I could only see large shapes and colors. Panicked, I started hyperventilating and woke Mark up. He dialed the bakery for me to tell them I wouldn't be coming into work. No one answered. We drove down to the bakery. Since I could only see shapes and colors, I held on to Mark's arm as he walked me through the production floor, looking for my manager. Once we found him and I told him I couldn't see, he sarcastically said, "Yeah, okay then. I guess you'd better go home." He thought I'd made the entire ordeal up because I didn't want to work there.

The next day, I went to see my eye doctor. We already knew the artificial lens that had been surgically placed in my eye years earlier had slipped out of position and was in the lower portion of my eye. However, what no one foresaw was that when I bent over, gravity moved it up and into my line of vision. There was only one specialist in Seattle who was the go-to expert for unusual and delicate cases such as mine, and he was on vacation for two weeks. Since this was my only "good" eye, I needed this specialist.

I entered one of the loneliest and most discouraging times of my sober life. I had no job and no insurance since the new job had a thirty-day waiting period. I couldn't drive. I could walk, but not across any busy streets because even though I could hear cars, I couldn't judge their distance or gauge how fast they were coming. I also couldn't see the "walk" signs. I am telling you this level of detail because this seemingly mundane part of my story holds life-changing information. I had been home for three or four days when Rika called with a bakery question, which I answered. Then, she asked me how the new job was going for me. I kept my answer short but relayed what had happened. She was kind and told me she was very sorry.

Life in the Word

Those days at home alone, while Mark was at work, were very dark for me. One morning, I picked up the TV remote and started pushing buttons from memory. As I clicked through the channels, I saw a woman's silhouette on the screen and what she said changed my life. I heard her ask, was I talking and complaining about my problems, or was I praising God because He was meeting my every need? Had I asked God to help me and then spent every waking moment thinking and talking about my problem? She suggested the issue was that my words were not aligned with the Word of God.

The woman was Joyce Meyer, and her teaching was "Me and My Big Mouth."

That is exactly what I was doing. I would talk about my problems, think about them, and think and talk about them some more. I knew the principle of whatever you magnify gets bigger. Now I saw it in action in my own life. In the days following, Mark set the VCR to record the show every day, and I watched each segment twice, once live and then the recording. I would pause on Scripture during my second viewing so I could find it in my Bible with my magnifying glass. This process is how I learned the chapters in my Bible, slowly. I had never actually opened my Bible before watching the show. Things began to turn around in my spirit. I bought a copy of the amplified Bible she was using to teach.

A week or so later, the phone rang, and it was Bob. Rika had told him what happened, and he'd called to see how I was doing. "Okay, I guess," I told him. "I'm waiting for surgery." He told me he could use some help in the office and asked me if I would be willing to come down to the company and help answer phones. He reminded me I could do that job with my eyes closed. We had a good laugh about it. He sent Rika to my house to pick me up for work. When I arrived at the bakery, Bob offered me my job back, under one condition. I had to stop looking for work. As desperate as I was to accept his offer, I pushed back a bit and told him he hadn't acted like he'd wanted me there. He agreed it might have looked that way. He reinstated my health insurance, and I had eye surgery. My vision was restored.

The Bigger Picture

Once I had a chance to think about it, here is what I think happened:

1. Bob wanted to be sure I was honest. His questioning of my integrity likely sprang from several hints Rika had made that I might be up to something. He admitted she had likely been after my job. After my absence, they both knew she wasn't qualified to do my job. She would later leave the company on good terms.

2. Bob may have pushed me to work under extreme conditions to see how I would hold up under pressure without him. He likely wanted to make sure if he sold me the bakery, I wouldn't give up when things got tough.

He hadn't counted on my resignation. He made mention that when I refused to sign the letter he had me write that day, he understood that if I wasn't willing to be dishonest for him, I wasn't likely to be dishonest to him. He hadn't intended it to be a test, but he did see it as a demonstration. I was about to owe him a lot of money. He needed to know he could trust me.

3. The things started happening when I got my Bible out and lined my words up with what I was asking of God. Think what you want about televangelists, but no other preacher was in my living room during the darkest point in my life. Thank you, Joyce. I love you.

"Do not despise these days of small beginnings, for the Lord rejoices to see the work begin."

— Zechariah 4:10 (NLT)

4. I learned not to make emotional decisions. Can you recall ever making a good emotional decision? Neither can I. Not having inquired with the Lord about it first, I pushed myself into that other bakery. Then I experienced the negative consequence: a work environment that was completely wrong for me. If we spend eight hours a night sleeping and eight hours a day at a job we despise, what can we expect the quality of the other eight hours in our day to be? How long can the strongest of people hold up before they bring a crummy attitude home? How long would it have been until the full-blown profanity I had worked so hard to remove came back into my conversations, and I started to think those dirty jokes were funny?

The other company continued to believe I made up the eye injury story, which hurt because it wasn't true. But it was just another of my emotional muscles getting exercised. I couldn't be responsible for how other people behaved. It was not my role to correct them. I had acted with as much integrity as I could. That needed to be enough. I clearly wasn't supposed to be there. I want to add that if God had led me there, I would have looked at this differently. I understand sometimes we are called to be in difficult situations. We may be the only light in a dark place. That wasn't my experience here. I had forced myself in.

I realized God was in control. He already knew everything that was going to happen. Had I already forgotten the miracles He had performed in pulling me out of the pit of drug despair, my first round of blindness, homelessness, and jail? I would not only return to my old position, but I would also one day soon become the owner. Oh, ye of little faith.

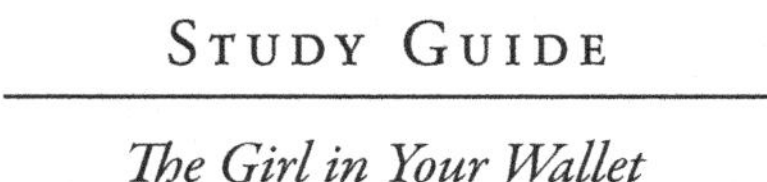

Chapter 11: Mistaking Motives

As I began to assert my personal values in the workplace, I had to confront someone in a position of authority. Do you have difficulty with confrontation? Explain.

____

____

____

If so, how can you begin to think of it as strengthening a muscle you haven't used before?

By placing Bob into the vacant father role in my life, I placed myself into the role of needy/abandoned daughter. Take a mental 360-degree view of the relationships in your life.

Is it possible you are trying to fill a hole left vacant by someone you needed? Jot some notes here to reflect on later.

My decision to change jobs was based on my fear of rejection and abandonment, not to further my career. Describe a time when you have reacted emotionally to a situation that had long term, unpleasant consequences. *(Helpful note: If there is someone who makes fun of you over these types of situations, they may not be a Safe Person. If you have someone who gently brings this situation up as a reminder not to repeat it, they are more likely to be a Safe Person.)*

My life went from bad to worse very quickly, and then I found hope through a television program. What principle did I learn that day?

Stopping the negative talk was just half the battle. What did I learn to think about instead of my problems?

How much power do you think negative self-talk has on your life?

God showed up when I was unemployed, uninsured, blind, discouraged, lonely, and hopeless. Describe a time God showed up for you when the situation seemed impossible.

Looking back now, what are some of the lessons you learned? Are they similar to the lessons I have outlined?

____

____

____

What are the five conclusions I made about this period and my experiences?

1. ____

2. ____

3. ____

4. ____

5. ____

Which one did you connect with the most? Why?

____

____

____

CHAPTER 12

Risking It All

"We often miss opportunity because it's dressed in overalls and looks like work."

—Thomas A. Edison

BOB BROUGHT UP the subject of selling me the business in the early summer of 2005. It was a casual conversation in his office, the door open. My immediate response was negative; I didn't have any money. He knew that already and said he had known and worked with me long enough to trust me to make payments. I was reeling with the possibilities and did two things when I left work that day. Each was met with a very different response.

I called Mark, and he was delighted. He repeated the mantra that he always knew he married me for my money; he just didn't think it would take this long. Then he went into all the ideas of what we could do in the future with our newfound wealth. Long accolades of how great I was at my job followed. Then we giggled about how if Bob only knew who we really were. I had not yet shed my previous identity, and I had a spouse who often seemed ready to remind me of our inferior social standing.

The second call was to my mother. I didn't know if buying the bakery would happen, but I was just so honored that Bob would think

I was smart enough and trustworthy enough to take over his business. I enthusiastically dialed her phone number, expecting she would be happy for me. If I had slowed down, I could have predicted her response based on history. Here's what happened:

Me: "Mom, Mom! Guess what? Bob offered to sell me the bakery!"

Mom: (nervous) "Oh, my gosh, Teresa, really? Do you think you should? (pause) Do you have someone who can run it for you?"

Here's the deal. I'd been running the bakery for Bob for nine years. He had relocated me across the state to do it. In all that time, she had not acknowledged what I did for a living and that I was capable. I held the phone receiver in my hand, just staring at it. I could hear her saying, "Hello? Hello?" It was a reminder of how disconnected she was from reality and me. She was locked into the poverty mindset. After I had time to process it all, it made me sad for her. She never had confidence in herself. So, it followed that she didn't have confidence in her children.

Learning to Stand on My Own

Mark and I would take advantage of the opportunity and purchase the company, knowing that Bob's asking price was likely nearly three times its value. I consulted a business advisor who was the first to point that out, and then a banker, who told me Bob might be taking advantage of me. What they didn't understand was that these things didn't happen to people like me. This was my shot, and I was going to take it. Bob carried the note himself, and we signed the deal in October 2005. Then something happened that, in all the excitement, I didn't plan for. Bob packed up his office and left. I had no idea how much of my value and self-worth was tied up in hearing him tell me I had done a good job. He left.

I was abandoned again. The office fell silent, and I had no idea what to do with myself. I felt scared, isolated, and depressed. The day

Bob walked out the door, I fell apart. I now could create whatever schedule I wanted. I could fill my days with...what? I seemed to have lost my identity. When I worked for Bob, I knew my responsibilities: to keep everything running, meet customer's deadlines, eliminate wasted product, and calculate payroll. I knew my main job was to keep Bob happy, and he seemed very pleased with my work. I liked knowing what was expected of me in day-to-day operations.

Now I was expected to make my own schedule and set my own priorities. The problem was I didn't have any. I had no idea how to structure my days. I was thrust into a vague, formless world in which I had no idea how to live. I went from meeting the demands of a manufacturing plant to being expected to understand how to read financial reports. I had never seen one before, and numbers are not my strength. When it was left up to me, I panicked and became depressed and isolated.

Finding My Place

When I took over as owner at the bakery, my role changed, as well as how people treated me. As general manager, I'd been able to buy time, saying I needed to ask the owner for permission to do or buy something. Now that I had all the purchasing authority for the business, I had finance people coming out of the woodwork seeking me out for equipment loans, vehicle loans, and to join their organizations. Without any formal education and having lived a sheltered life, I did not speak "business language." I was overwhelmed by "smart people" who spoke of return on investment (ROI), working capital, and diversification. I had no idea what any of that meant. What I knew how to do was make high-quality bread and cookies, run a tight production schedule, and be a tough negotiator. I could not hold up my side of the conversation with these people. I began hiding from them.

The company's banker was also from Spokane, and we had gone

to the same high school. He was very involved with many local civic, community, and alumni organizations. He asked if a local newsletter could interview me for a "local girl makes good" piece and take a photo for my former high school. I had finished the tenth grade, but only three to four months of that year had been at that high school. I had also gone to several alternative schools. When they looked up my transcripts, they would know that, but I needed to keep my relationship with the banker in good standing. In my mind, my history could cost me everything. Whether that was true or not, I didn't know. I was paranoid and felt jobs were on the line—mine and forty other employees'.

I stalled the banker for a long time until he eventually stopped asking me for the interview. I'm sure he was discouraged and confused by my resistance to getting more exposure for the bakery since most businesses want it. Not me, though. I had something to hide. I felt fraudulent. I feared "being found out." I was leading a double life, and it was exhausting.

What made my situation even worse was I had a husband at home who acted as if he'd just won the lottery. I would come home at the end of the day and listen to Mark pitching multiple ways to lead the high life at the company's expense. He had grand ideas about taking vacations and expensing the trips to the company. Was there an equipment manufacturer in Vegas? A bakery tour in San Francisco? Different styles of bread to look at as research? He continued to tell people he knew he had married me for my money; he just didn't think it would take this long. In hindsight, I realize he wasn't kidding. It seems he had more faith in me than I had in myself. I was further driven to succeed, not wanting to risk disappointing him. We were in constant conflict; our values were not aligned.

The pressure was intense at work and especially at home. I could not get away from it. The stress was unraveling me. Scared and desperate, I again decided to make an emotional decision. Three months after taking over the bakery, I hired a sales and distribution manager. I remember thinking how smart he was. I was very impressed with his management experience and allowed him to have more and more control in the company. But I had an uneasy feeling in my gut about many of his decisions. Nothing was technically wrong with them, but I had internal conflicts I could not identify. Yet I stayed silent and gave him full rein because, looking back, I again sought someone to make my decisions for me. I was so tired, and my self-esteem was so low that after all those many victories the Lord had brought me through, I was focused on how unqualified I was instead of God's sufficiency.

Study Guide

The Girl in Your Wallet

Chapter 12: Risking It All

How did Mark's response to the news of buying the bakery differ from my mother's?

____

____

____

How were they similar, although, perhaps, expressed differently?

____

____

____

Feeling like a "fraud" or "fear of being found out" is common as we strive for more. Have you ever experienced "imposter syndrome"? If so, did you feel it was a lack of confidence or competence? Explain.

CHAPTER 13

It Looked Good on Paper

"When you find yourself in a hole, stop digging."
—Will Rogers

I WAS SPINNING, literally, emotionally, mentally. I walked mindlessly at the office from one desk to the next with no purpose or destination in mind. My behavior did not incite faith in my leadership with the employees. I wasn't in any danger of them turning on me; however, none of them wanted to be in my shoes. None of them would step up to be an armchair quarterback that day.

We bit off more than we could chew. If we hadn't heard the phrase "It looked good on paper" already, we would have coined it ourselves. The launch had failed, and the repercussions were compounding quickly.

We had developed a fantastic cookie that met the definition of high protein, clean-label, non-GMO, and the timing was right in our Seattle market. This cookie was excellent, and I'd had no problem selling it to a warehouse store in large clamshell packaging.

Therein lay the problem. Approved in multiple locations throughout the Pacific Northwest, this was a high-volume account. While the plan looked good on paper, we didn't build enough downtime for the glitches that come with work and life. We didn't build-in enough grace. When we shipped the first order, we were already behind. But we were also sampling in the locations, and members were buying far more than we anticipated. Low inventory/high demand. Disaster.

In our bakery, the term "in stock" did not apply. Almost everything was made fresh, except for orders for foodservice customers that ordered in cases on pallets. By the time we as managers met to discuss the problem, tomorrow's order was incomplete, and the shortage would roll forward and grow day by day. The stress of the situation reached the production floor, and in the chaos, the baker was distracted and overbaked multiple racks, each containing more than fifty-six dozen cookies. We couldn't sell them. The pressure was crushing me.

I dialed the phone to call Bob, presumably to get his advice as the previous owner. We had stayed in touch, and he consulted for me, but less often as I had settled into my new position as owner. As I dialed the phone, it felt a little more like asking for fatherly advice.

I laid out the problem, and Bob asked several relevant questions, but of course, he wouldn't tell me what to do. It was no longer his company. I had all the information. He suggested I make the best decision I could, cut back on expenses to survive the financial impact, lay-off non-essentials, accept the outcome, and rebuild. "Teresa, you know what to do; you just don't like it. Make the decisions you will be proud of yourself for when you look back at this later."

Our conversation shifted at that point. I apologized. I apologized for all the times I had sat in on "boss bashing" conversations with my fellow employees. I was suddenly aware of my suggesting it wasn't that hard, implying Bob was either selfish or just lazy. I knew he was uncomfortable, and it was pretty quiet on his end. He finally said he didn't think an apology was necessary since he wasn't aware it had happened. "I know I happened. The apology is to make things right with myself."

Owning your own business is a lonely endeavor. It wasn't as big a problem until we decided to grow. The more we did and added more moving parts and people, the smaller my world got. There are many perks when things are going well, but you can quickly lose them. This was one of the times of loss. Did I mention this was early 2008? It was about to get a lot worse.

As I was stumbling around the office mindlessly, I saw a prepared bank deposit on my office manager's desk. I grabbed it, found my keys, and hopped in the car. Change of scenery, fresh air, couldn't hurt.

From the bank parking lot, I called Barb, my second AA sponsor. A rapid-fire release of partial sentences accompanied by hyperventilating followed. But something else was happening, too, and I was spitting out things that didn't have anything to do with the specific cookie issue. As I told her what my problem was, I was adding items and making them an emergency. "I don't have time for an oil change. Restaurant X still has an open invoice. The dogs needed to go to the groomer." Wait? What? Whoa....

God bless the woman. In her calm voice, she showed concern and asked for clarification. I must have viewed her questions as suggestions in my frenzy because I was smacking them down like a game of whack-a-mole. She gave me an assignment, which I was to complete right there in the bank parking lot, and when finished, I was to call her back.

"Teresa, do you have a pen and paper? Okay, I want you to write down all the things swimming around in your head. Bullet points. Don't worry about spelling or penmanship. Topics. Not sentences. I expect you to do this very quickly since they are all at the forefront of your mind. It doesn't matter if you write the same thing more than once. Write. Write until you have slowed down and run out of topics. Then take a deep breath and call me back. Can you do that?"

It didn't take long. Deep breath, slow exhale. Dial the phone. "Now, I want you to go back and cross off all the ones that are a normal part of life and can wait. Which ones are not urgent? When you have finished, take a deep breath and call me back."

My heart rate was slowing. She was giving me a tangible exercise that was tapping into my visual learning style. I could see myself releasing anxiety on those torn notebook pages with a frantic scribble. A doctor could have written them, but I could read them, and it allowed me to see inside my soul. When I called her back the second time, she asked which items were left, which ones needed confronting. The most unpleasant ones, of course.

I still didn't know what to do when I returned to work, but the answer came as I turned the corner and faced my office door. I had missed calls from the broker and the warehouse store buyer. On each, the office staff had created a tally of how many times they had called. It was time to admit defeat.

I found a larger, better-equipped bakery to make the product for the customer and shipped them the thousands of dollars of ingredients, packaging supplies, and labels, and gave them my recipe. They were to pay for the items when they satisfied the customer, which never happened. The customer didn't like their version and canceled all future orders—a complete loss for us.

Because we had sold bread to the warehouse store for more than two decades, that business continued. They would not purchase cookies from us again. The relationship with the broker was irreparably damaged. He wanted assurance we could meet the quality and quantity of future orders. I could assure him of neither.

Those steps took care of what was happening outside of our building. There was an internal fall-out as well. One manager felt I gave up too quickly; he never forgave me, and there was nothing I could do about that. I no longer had unrest about my course of action. It just sucked.

I still had to meet payroll for the product that never sold. My paycheck slashed, I called the bank and told them I could not make the payments on my home and listed it as a short sale. I delivered my car back to the lot I had purchased it from and made payments on the money I owed. We were driving huge bags of burnt product to the garbage dump. We were incredibly humbled, but we would survive.

What did I learn from this? Count the cost.

> *"Suppose one of you wants to build a tower. Won't you first sit down and estimate the cost to see if you have enough money to complete it?"*
>
> —Luke 14:28

It looked good on paper and would have put us on the map, but I had not fully considered the endeavor, nor did I trust the uneasy feeling in my gut. Again. Our team was so excited, and everyone had loved the finished product. I had got caught up in the excitement and wanted to make them happy. I probably had some ego involved. We were a small company with a big opportunity.

I am responsible for my own decisions and will live with their consequences—so will you. When this project went wrong, I was alone. No one was knocking on my door, offering to help shoulder the financial loss, nor should they have been. I need to consider the source of advice when making significant decisions. I should have been calling my fellow business owners and asking for their input. Be mindful of where you are turning for advice. Perhaps reach out to people who have survived a similar experience. Ask them what they did right and wrong, both of which are equally valuable.

It's all fun and games until somebody has to pay for it. I was financially responsible, and there is no line between personal and financial repercussions for an owner. I wasn't even eligible for unemployment benefits. It was a big lesson that almost put me out of business.

My sponsor gave me a tool I could repeatedly use in many areas of my life to address anxiety and decision-making difficulties. Making a list using these steps and format has been very helpful—brain dump first, then sort and prioritize. It calmed the frenzy. Have you ever been under so much stress that you decide it's a good time to move or remodel the house? Me too. I have come to believe it is a scramble to control something, at least one thing, when everything else is out of control. It's also a very bad idea.

I may have added the minor issues to the list next to my colossal problem in an attempt to dilute it. Or shift my focus. Perhaps a survival mechanism kicked in, I don't know, but I have noticed my tendency to do the same thing in other situations. I have to remind myself to keep the main thing as the main thing.

I appreciate that in the phone call with my former boss, I recalled myself as an employee criticizing him for his decisions when I knew nothing about what he dealt with daily. It was very arrogant of me, and I am grateful for this humbling experience. Finally, if you have someone to thank or apologize to, do it.

Many years later, as I moved business records into a storage unit, I found a box of Bob's accounting files. In it, I saw two sets of loan documents. One set was for the third mortgage he had taken on his home and one for the loan he made to the company with the money. I had been in his employ when the transaction had taken place, but I'd had no idea we were in financial trouble. He was taking care of business. I am pleased I apologized that day.

If you feel the tug to apologize, consider doing it with haste. Coming back to it at a later time often requires filling in all the backstory and can make things more awkward. The opportunity to speak these words to my former boss came suddenly, and I took it. I am glad I did.

Chapter 13: It Looked Good on Paper

Recall a time when your efforts failed and left you spinning emotionally. What were the circumstances?

If you called someone for counsel, how much thought did you give to which person you called? Did you choose wisely?

Is there a disturbing reality you are avoiding at this moment because you wish it weren't true? If so, what is avoiding the situation costing you? What is the cost of your inaction? (Example: daily turmoil, short-tempered with others, etc.)

Can you think of a time when you've misjudged someone's actions or motives to find yourself in their position later? Were your initial assumptions correct, or do you now have more empathy? Explain.

CHAPTER 14

Seeing Results

"When you change the way you look at things, the things you look at change."

— Dr. Wayne Dyer

I HAD BUSINESS professionals telling me I was a natural at being an entrepreneur, but we were coasting on the systems Bob had put in place. I was skilled in many areas, but he did not teach me how to operate the finances. I began to receive warnings from our banker and accountant about our weakening financial strength, and it became tougher to pay the bills each week. I focused only on product quality and customer service, and it wasn't long before the bank shut down our credit line. I didn't understand any of it. We were forced to enter into a factoring agreement.

Factoring is a transaction in which a business sells its invoices, or receivables, to a third-party financial company known as a "factor." The factor then collects payment on those invoices from the business's customers. Factoring is known in some industries as "accounts receivable financing." We no longer had immediate access to our incoming payments, and the operating capital the service provided cost the company $4,000 a month. We were going under financially, and I had no idea what to do about it. I took a 25 percent pay cut, made a short sale on my home, and returned my Acura to the car lot. I borrowed a car until I could save enough money to buy a little Kia.

One morning in 2012, after months of struggling, I had reached the end of myself. Sitting in my car in the driveway before work, I shouted loudly at God, "What? What do you want from me? You said you would never leave me, but I'm not feeling you in *any* of this! What do you want from me? Why won't you let me quit?" It took a lot of energy since it came from somewhere deep inside. Exhausted, I sat and listened to the rain pelt on the car roof. Then quietly, I heard two things in my spirit. The first was, "Finally." I was finally willing to hand it over to God. The second thought was of a bakery consultant who had called me six months earlier. I had no examples of how a typical business operated since this was my first real job, and I was left alone most of the time to figure it out. Still sitting in my driveway before work, I decided to do whatever it took to turn the company around. I determined I would do the hard things. I dialed the bakery consultant's phone number, and by midday, I was twenty miles away, having lunch with a man who had spent thirty-five successful years in my industry. I hired him as a consultant on the spot.

Dennis never told me what to do, but he taught me what I needed to know. I'd had the capacity to learn those things all along and could have if I had not hidden from my new position and the problems. We uncovered some troubling employee practices and either released them or left before we got too close. We analyzed customer data and apologetically discontinued business with non-profitable customers. We dropped small production run items. Once our consultant showed me how to look at the information and how to run the company, I began to realize I had been capable the entire time. I had looked at myself and seen only the high school dropout, the convicted felon, and the drug addict, not understanding that I was no longer any of those things. It wasn't until I reached the end of myself and submitted it all to God that I would have the privilege of watching what He would do through me. It was another example of the gift of desperation. We reached a point of profitability in 2014 and were able to gain a traditional bank line of credit and end the relationship with the factoring company.

In hindsight, I see how buying a bakery when I was still fragile in my self-esteem was a huge leap for me. Looking back, I can see my accomplishments were substantial, and as my company successfully grew, so did my confidence. In the twelve years between 2005 and 2017, the following things occurred:

- Annual revenue increased from $1.9 million to $3.6 million, with distribution to Washington, Oregon, and Alaska.
- Growth. We gained twenty-plus employees and expanded to a 17,500 square-foot facility.
- Diversification. We directed our sales efforts to create a 50/50 balance between direct store delivery (DSD) and food-service distributors, with bi-annual reviews. Essentially, we developed and maintained a balance of local self-reliance and long-haul distributors. From there, we enlarged our quantity of distribution customers. I also created three new management positions and hired experienced management staff at industry-competitive wages.
- Exceptional customer service. It was common for customers to speak directly to me when discontinuing service. They expected me to try to change their minds. However, after asking them their reason for leaving, I'd graciously respect their decision without too much inquiry and wish them well. Many customers came back to us after a time.
- I hired a veteran of the baking industry as an operations manager. My two-year commercial baking degree would not keep us competitive in the marketplace, and I knew it. I had taken the bakery as far as I could with my limited schooling. We needed automation and experience.

- I increased the company's entry-level wage by 18 percent and offered a reimbursement program for employees' English as a Second Language (ESL) classes. New employees received bus passes.

- Custom Research and Development (R&D). I personally created and sold unique bread and cookie items to major warehouse stores, high-end private label stores, and food-service distributors. I worked directly with executive chefs at restaurants to create signature menu items. I never reached a point in my career when I stopped wanting to make baked goods with my own hands.

- We created a professional development budget for our management staff for baking demonstrations, annual baking conventions, out-of-state equipment demonstrations, Dale Carnegie Training, and one-week intensive leadership conferences.

- I created a highly specialized R&D ordering system to qualify customers' requests before the production run. Spreadsheets had limited options to ensure a profitable sample before beginning a production run.

- Account receivables were collected, on average, in fourteen days. To benefit the company and customers, I often negotiated delivery modifications in lieu of price increases.

- I secured and paid in full nearly $700,000 in bank loans, paid off bakery note at an estimated three-times its value, all while surviving a $4,000 a month factoring agreement for several years.

- All those years of stress and anxiety at the bakery took their toll, and although I had found peace knowing we had brought the company back from the brink of ruin to profitability and abundance, God let me know my time there was complete. On December 31, 2016, I signed the final sale documents and walked out the door for the last time. I was brought to tears when I had the privilege of walking into my church's finance office and giving them my donation from the sale. The entire journey with the company being completed with an act of obedience just levels me. I am not worthy, yet He loves me.

"Whoever said money can't buy happiness hasn't given enough away yet."

—Anonymous

Study Guide

The Girl in Your Wallet

Chapter 14: Seeing Results

Life challenges us with defining moments (usually stressful!) that demand growth. What was God waiting to hear from me?

____

____

____

With "surrender" came the answer to my problem—hire a bakery consultant. How have you experienced an answer to prayer when you stopped trying to solve the problem yourself?

____

____

____

I looked at myself and saw only the high school dropout, the convicted felon, and the drug addict. Joyce K. had told me early on not to compare my insides to everyone else's outsides, but twenty years later, I was still doing it. Do you struggle in this area? Do you find it challenging to accept a compliment and, possibly, wonder why the person is sucking up? Explain.

My inner dialogue and labels I carried for myself, and my career accomplishments did not line up and created a conflicted energy other people felt. Being difficult to "get to know" or "stand-offish" were not uncommon observations from around me. Consider your achievements, both personal and professional, against what you see in the mirror and the descriptive labels you have for yourself. How big is the divide?

Do you have a big dream that is perhaps beyond your current abilities or level of courage, one that could only be accomplished with God? Take a moment to write it here, no matter how far-fetched it may seem. You do not have to share your answer, but I think there is excellent value in admitting it to yourself on paper. (One of mine has been writing this book!)

CHAPTER 15

The Exchange System

"We are the average of the five people we spend the most time with."

—Jim Rohn

MOTIVATIONAL SPEAKER JIM Rohn famously said that we are the average of the five people we spend the most time with. We absorb our environments, good or bad. How much more so when we are children looking at the adults in our lives and modeling their behavior. If I spend time with pessimists, I find myself complaining more. If I spent time with optimists, I see more opportunities and kindness in the world.

When I first considered this concept, my go-to response was that I couldn't control where I spend most of my time. I can't control other people, including my coworkers, family, church members, volunteer teams, etc. I had also recently began leading Bible-based life skills classes at the women's prison and they certainly can't determine who is in their immediate space. They go where they are assigned. Since so much of our lives is without control in this area, we need to be intentional with the rest.

As I was preparing a lesson for the prison, the concept from Jim Rohn took center stage, dominating my thoughts. I was working with an established curriculum, so I had a topic, but whenever I sat down at my computer, the concept continued to dominate my mind space. Day after day, I struggled, and I had a deadline looming. I wrote a separate lesson for the class that week and let this idea continue to unfold.

I drew a circle on a sheet of paper. Inside the circle, I wrote words that described the negative beliefs I held about myself in the past—the ones I felt could be relatable. Not all of them originated from me, but they had been offered up by people who had played a role in my life at some point. I latched on to them, making them my own and allowed them to become a deeply rooted part of my self-perception. They were my identity.

My list included: thief, liar, selfish, unfaithful, failure, manipulator, worthless. In the depths of my being, I used the word murderer for those abortions; that is how I had come to speak to myself about them. As a young Christian in my clean and sober life, deep down inside, I still believed the old me was the real me. The conflict between my inner beliefs and my outward behavior caused conflicted energy. I was unstable.

These labels are no longer active, and I no longer use them in my internal dialogue. But, where and when did they cease? How? The "average of five people" concept had provoked thought, and while I thought I was writing lessons that day, it turned into a much longer endeavor.

Wikipedia defines "revelation knowledge" this way: "In religion and theology, revelation is the revealing or disclosing of some form of truth or knowledge through communication with a deity or other supernatural entity or entities." God was giving me revelation knowledge, and I allowed it time to unfold.

I looked at the circle I had drawn and the descriptive words I had used as my identity firmly locked inside it. I added arrowheads to the line of the circle representing a clockwise motion. They had been a tornado of negativity spinning in mind, constantly in motion fueled by anxiety and insecurity. I imagine it much like the cartoon character of the Tasmanian Devil, rapidly spinning with bizarre unpredictable behavior flinging off in all directions. There were peaks of eruption that often weren't triggered by any circumstances at all. I was always spinning.

I drew an outer circle very near the first representing the person I might spend the most time with. On it, I drew arrowheads circling the same direction as the first. In those early sober and newly Christian years, this would have been my second husband, Mark. He agreed with the words I used to identify myself, but I had to take ownership of him having this opinion. *After all, that is how I introduced myself to him—laying out all my weaknesses to someone I had just met.*

Four more circles representing the remaining people I spent the most time with all with arrows of their own, and I had now drawn a seemingly impenetrable cylinder. I had locked myself into this negative cycle and surrounded myself with people who reinforced it. Ironically, I was quite comfortable there. In some ways, it felt nice to be in the company of those who understood me. Comfortable, yes. But not good for me.

"Show me your friends and I will show you your future."

—Unknown

The completed drawing I now held in my hand showed held self-destructive words locked inside five circles—all five in motion, each with the arrow's tips pointing out. The visual familiarity became instantly clear.

It was the spiral of barbed wire surrounding the prison.

I wanted to break out, to grow. I was starting to do well in my job and school, but I reminded myself not to think too highly of myself. That wasn't godly, after all. If I did muster the courage to stretch myself and try something new, I need not look too far for someone to point out the activity or goal was likely outside my ability. *It wasn't for people like us*. Although I loved these people and they loved me, I was getting restless.

The breakthrough came when I began to read my Bible. I had been a Christian for many years and attended church services regularly, but when I opened what sometimes felt like a dusty, old book, I didn't glean what the pastors could on Sunday morning or on television. As I grew more familiar with the order of the chapters and the pastor said to turn to a particular verse, I could sometimes get there before they started reading. The words were beginning to make sense while the pastor was teaching; this was a start, but at home, I was still struggling. They were words on a page, a lot of them not part of our everyday language. Until... until I heard Hebrews 11:6: "and without faith, it is impossible to please God because anyone who comes to Him must first believe He exists and that *He rewards those who diligently seek Him*." (NIV)

I had given my life to Jesus to the best of my ability at the time, but I was hungry for more. I had no idea what to do and was too scared to ask anyone for help. I had enough people laughing at me. Social anxiety was controlling much of my outward behavior at church, sliding in after the singing started and leaving as the pastor was winding down his message, but I could control what I did on my own. I decided the "reward" for me in Hebrews 11:6 was the ability to hear from God myself, without always needing an interpreter. I had faith that He would give me the ability to understand *if I sought it diligently*.

So, I stumbled my way through reading the Bible on my own. I stopped trying to hurry through the Bible during church service to find the next place we were reading and just jotted down the verse so I could come back to it later. In the time it took to drive home, the verse had lost its clarity and relevance, but I kept at it. I pinned my key verse of Hebrews 11:6 next to the kitchen sink and considered it many times each day.

"I meditate on your precepts and consider your ways."
—Psalm 119:5

God's Word is reliable. I began to have a basic understanding of His desire for a relationship with me, but I had a big setback when it came to the descriptive words the Bible used for me. They did not match the ones I used for myself, the ones locked inside my circles. My self-talk told me I was beyond redemption and that I deserved to be in pain, but then where was this hunger coming from?

I had a decision to make. Either I believed the Bible or I didn't. I wasn't concerned about being held responsible for what I didn't understand. But we're not talking about deep theology here. We are discussing God's love for His children, which is consistent throughout the book. Only in hindsight can I tell you that is how I broke free, and it took a great deal of time. If I was the "average of the five people I spend the most time with," *I was going to have to spend more time with God.*

When I invited Jesus into my heart, it provided a crack in the cylinder holding my beliefs. If I didn't want to carry the labels anymore, I wouldn't get far without His power to keep moving and His forgiveness when I fell short. I found it difficult to release something without leaving a void that would suck something in to fill the space like a vacuum. I would continue to absorb my environment. It needed to be an exchange system.

For example, when I tried to deal with being selfish on my own, it seemed like it activated more of it. It required a shift in thinking. I needed to focus on what I wanted, what would fill that space. Instead of repeating the mantra "not to be selfish," I could use my new tools—faith, prayer, the Bible, and willingness to seek out His desire. What did God's Word say about me? I learned to use a Bible concordance and looked up the opposite of selfish. I looked up references to generosity.

I can't be selfish and generous at the same time. Generosity is giving, helping, and even just being kind. Am I unselfish all the time?

Not a chance, but it widened the crack in the circle surrounding my beliefs. Selfish slipped out (and back in occasionally), and generosity slipped in filling the newly vacated space. I liked myself more with this exchange and delighted in what I was learning. *God was rewarding me as I diligently sought Him.* The Bible is full of His promises, and since "He is no respecter of persons" (Acts 10:34), it is available to all of us.

As the voice of God became clearer and more important to me, it became easier to believe He saw these things in me. It seems the way I viewed myself didn't change His opinion at all. Over time, the five people who compose my inner circle have changed. Some left exclaiming how boring or goody-goody I was. One suggested I was taking this religion thing too far. Others I just spent less time around, and it made more space in my life. Space for people who are healthier for me and who challenge me to grow. Another exchange system. Since we naturally gravitate to those who are like us, I was attracted to generous people. I was intentional not to let random people fill those vital five spaces; they are held by those who encourage me to be all God has called me to be and comfort and encourage me when I step out and fail.

Study Guide

The Girl in Your Wallet

Chapter 15: The Exchange System

Without judgment, list today's date and the five people you spend the most time with.

1. ______________________________________

2. ______________________________________

3. ______________________________________

4. ______________________________________

5. ______________________________________

Rate your willingness to do the exercise of listing the descriptive words you use for yourself.

Low 1 2 3 4 5 High

If you were to hear these words in your circles spoken in an audible voice, would the voice be yours, or would it belong to someone else? Whose is the dominant voice?

Have you ever thought of the Bible as an "outdated" or a "dusty old book"?

What are you willing to let go of to make more space for God and positive influences?

NOTE: The experience outlined above resulted in the logo you will find on the final pages of this book.

CHAPTER 16

Transferrable Skills

"There will always be someone who can't see your worth. Don't let it be you."
—Mel Robbins

I HAD A therapist tell me I was successful in business because I had never been taught boundaries. Culturally, I thought that was a negative trait except in the context of creative problem-solving. Since I hadn't been taught boundaries, I went through life sometimes believing there weren't any. I can tell you without a shadow of a doubt that God has turned that into a blessing. I am very aware that not all of my ideas are good ones, but they can be very creative. Sometimes we can take a piece of this and a bit of that and come up with something. I was so busy being insecure about having no job experience that I completely overlooked that I had acquired some transferrable skills. I had received my education on the streets, but it was indeed an education.

I was unaware that one of my greatest strengths was misunderstood by my coworkers until I learned to identify it properly for myself. I am a great troubleshooter. Bob would bring me ideas of policies or procedures he thought about implementing and discuss them with me. Since I had so much experience misusing well-intended programs, I could show him the gaps that needed to be filled so no one could take advantage of them. My coworkers thought I was shooting down their suggestions. That wasn't it. I intended to make the programs sustainable and protected against abuse. Once we understood this, we worked together as a team to have fantastic, well-rounded brainstorming sessions. At one time, I had used my skills for evil, but now I could use them for good!

I came into business ownership focused on what I believed I lacked. I had street smarts and survival skills, and you cannot learn those at business college. I was blessed with the experience that had taught me how to squirm out from under angry customers and, ultimately, reach pleasant resolutions, and my intuition was honed enough to spot a "BS" story from twenty yards away.

My early years at the bakery were not without their challenges. A hostile coworker was not at all unlike an abrasive, potentially violent person in my drug circles. Certainly, those of you who have done time have had to navigate around someone aggressive to maintain some level of peace and stay out of the hole (solitary confinement). That is an example of endurance, and it is a transferrable skill. You might say you perform well under pressure. Negotiating solutions is called brainstorming. How about keeping an on-time schedule required by an institution or transitional housing? We call that punctuality and dependability. Can you think of a time you needed something, explained its importance, and why someone should help? You have done sales, my friend. Take *all* dishonesty and manipulation out of it, and the principles remain the same. Define the need and provide the solution. Sometimes, I think the main difference between manipulation and marketing is motive. Manipulation is self-seeking and often deceptive. Marketing benefits both parties.

My previous experiences had also allowed me to become very adept at accurately reading a situation and acting accordingly. In extreme cases, this skill kept me alive. In the business world, this might be termed emotional intelligence.

These are valued skills. The challenge is for you to recognize them about yourself, word them in a way that shows you are an asset, and then get yourself and your list of attributes in front of a hiring manager. When hired, prove yourself. I only have my own experience from which to draw, but when I focused on what I did well and set out to learn what I didn't, my work changed from being a job to a career. I could then begin to flourish. I became a vital member of the team and then moved on to lead the team.

Toward the end of my career, I found being invited to speak to a group of aspiring entrepreneurs to be both ironic and very rewarding. It was a small group; many of its members had been very successful in careers at Boeing and Microsoft and were now following their dreams of owning their own businesses. They were intelligent, educated people, and I could not imagine what I could possibly offer them. Yet, there they were, listening intently, staying late to ask me questions after class. As one gentleman put it, "I have been studying this for years. I want to hear from someone who has been in the trenches and lived to tell the tale."

In 2012, I joined a women's MBA association. You already know I do not hold that level of education. I joined because they had an open membership. I joined because they let me. I sought out other businesswomen who could (and would) teach me what I didn't know.

At a formal event in Seattle, a Boeing executive of twenty years shared a tidbit I could use. In essence, she suggested we recognize our strengths and weaknesses equally but not treat them equally. Don't let your weaknesses become "fatal flaws." Chances are your coworkers and managers are already aware of yours. Acknowledge your weak spots for yourself, bring them up to an acceptable level, and then focus your energy on your strengths. If you don't, that area you dismiss as small and insignificant could be your undoing.

Apply for Everything, Abuse Nothing

In addition to identifying your transferrable skills, make the best use of opportunities. Apply for *everything*: When I was released from inpatient treatment, I was required to report to probation and outpatient treatment. As I partially mentioned earlier, both were great resources for finding help. I was greatly impacted by Project Self-Sufficiency at the community college. What I haven't told you is that by its class description, I didn't qualify. It was designed as a welfare-to-work program for single mothers. When it was suggested to me by my caseworker, I listed all the reasons I couldn't go. I was not a single mother, and my child was not with me. He said, "Teresa, I want you to try to get out of your own way. I know the woman who created this class. She is expecting your call." Was I afraid of success or afraid of failure? I am not sure. I was certainly in the habit of disqualifying myself.

Use wisdom and guidance in accepting admission to a class or a job: When I overloaded my schedule, it meant I had unrealistic expectations about my time and commitment ability. It created unnecessary stress and made me feel bad that I couldn't keep up. Pray about it. Ask your trusted advisors. Be realistic.

Abuse Nothing: This has been one of my greatest challenges. Long ingrained in me was the idea that you must take what you can get whenever you can (see my earlier bouts with welfare fraud). To me, program abuse was whenever I manipulated the information to get what I wanted. In the early years of my sobriety, that meant knowingly leaving out pertinent information to qualify for something. (By the way, I don't think God blesses that.) It might have meant overstating my skills for a program or accepting gas money or a bus pass I no longer needed. My suggestion is to be forthcoming, and if the source still wants to help you, you can accept it with your conscience intact.

If you need public assistance, get it. There is no shame in that. But when we manipulate information beyond the need, I think we sacrifice a part of our soul. For me, there was a different value in money earned versus money given. They both paid the rent, but my sense of worth and self-esteem went up when I knew I worked for the money. You will have to decide for yourself.

After so many years of hiring for the bakery, I would add one more example from an employer's perspective. Be honest. If you really can't begin work at 4:00 a.m., please say so. If you get caught up in the moment and accept a position and realize later it won't work, call them. It takes about ten seconds of being uncomfortable on the phone to let them know. Please know what it can do to your spirit to be a no-show. I have done it so many times, and every time I reflect on it, I get that sinking, disappointed feeling. Ugh. Learn to do the hard thing, and you will learn how to have respect for yourself.

Do the Hard Thing

Will it be hard? Yes. Without question. I would still like to suggest some of you have already experienced hard, but without a good outcome. I don't have to know what you experienced before incarceration. I can guess it was hard. I know the arrest process was hard, and I know it was hard every day in the institution. Turning your life around will also be hard, and not everyone you know will be a cheerleader. I, for one, was tired enough to go for it. I was tired of looking over my shoulder, tired of being homeless, tired of being strip-searched, tired of being reminded of my identity as a criminal, and tired of being deemed unsuitable by society. I had endured *hard* all my life and had no peace or anything to be proud of. I became willing to do hard and scared for a shot at a different life. I put one foot in front of the other, looked only at the five feet in front of me, and when I surrendered my life to Him, God met me there. I became willing to view failures as teachable moments (embarrassment won't kill you, I promise) and take my risks in a new direction.

Chapter 16: Transferrable Skills

Street smarts and survival skills cannot be learned at business college, but they are transferrable skills! What specific skills did I possess that were helpful in business? List as many as you can.

"Learn to do the hard thing, and you learn how to have respect for yourself." What hard thing are you avoiding right now? How does it make you feel when you think about it? (Do a mental body scan here. Did your pulse quicken? Dread in the pit of your stomach? Does your neck tense up? etc.) Is putting it off solving the problem? Is it creating physical distress?

List several examples of your transferable skills. What talents and abilities have your unique life experiences taught you? If you have trouble with this exercise, I invite you to ask a Safe Person what they see in you. (Resist the urge to interrupt or argue back!)

In what circumstances have you been offered an opportunity, and declined because you weren't qualified or felt you didn't deserve it? If you have used the same reasons before, what are they? List some here.

In the example you listed above, is the critical voice yours or the voice of someone who influenced you in your youth? Please think about this objectively and without judgment. Who is speaking?

In the Chapter 6 questions, we looked at the definition of tired. What did you list being "tired of"? Does your answer relate to the issue you are avoiding?

CHAPTER 17

Releasing the Power of Your Past

"You can get the monkey off your back,
but the circus never leaves town."
—Ann Lamott

SOMETIMES I DON'T realize how much pain I'm in until I get out of it.

Alongside increased responsibility in my career and success in my company, I realized the main things Mark and I had in common were deep personal hurts in our youth and the experience of being arrested together. Our marriage continued to fall apart. Eventually, I had to face that our constant battle of wills and our differences in core values and behaviors were not consistent with my view of a respectful marriage. I had trusted him with our finances, which in and of itself wasn't a bad thing. But it was a big mistake that I never looked at them again. When I added in his lack of remorse and his perspective that our failing marriage was all my fault, I was done. I stopped trying to learn everything that had been going on and just accepted that the only thing I knew for sure was there would always be more I didn't know. We had been living on the memory of our initial attraction and the shared experience of being arrested. As my hunger and thirst for the Word and honest living increased, Mark made it clear that my desire to grow in Christ was not something he supported. I was miserable and had been for most of our sixteen years together.

I found out that being alone in a marriage is far worse than being alone.

The Sunday morning arguments we had as I tried to get out the door to go to church led to another huge regret. One day, I stopped trying. I stopped going to church. I was constantly conflicted between what the Bible said about me being a new person and what those around me said to remind me of where I came from. I was further conflicted about the concept of submitting to your husband when I did not respect Mark. My best advice to any woman is to be careful whom you hitch your wagon to. It's far too easy to get derailed when the person closest to you doesn't share your values or encourages you to stay small, so they are more comfortable.

The Crab Mentality

After Mark and I separated and began divorce proceedings, I had lunch with a dear friend. After lunch with him and his wife, we dropped her off for a hair appointment, and we went to a grocery store. I thought that was odd because he knew I was in crisis. Why were we shopping? He stayed calm, and while driving, he asked me if I had ever gone crabbing. He explained that if you caught one crab and placed him in a five-gallon bucket, you must put a lid on it, or he will climb out. If you catch more than one, you do not need a cover because the second, presumably weaker crab won't let him out. He will hold the other down. My friend turned to me and said, "Mark is never going to allow you to be all God has called you to be. It is your decision whether to keep him in your bucket, but he is not going to let you out."

Backsliding

After the divorce (and before I sold my business), I left the home Mark and I shared and moved into a two-bedroom apartment near work. The apartment was half-underground, so it was also very dark. In combination with Seattle's gloomy overcast days, the place did nothing for my depression, and it was about to get worse. My front door directly faced my neighbors' door, and our patios were also right next to one another. Let's just say I could hear them interact.

They were a young couple in their twenties with two young children, and what I could hear were the sounds of him beating her. I knew those sounds all too well. Through muffled cries, I could also hear her sobbing, "I'm sorry," and his very clear "Why do you have to be so stupid?" I spent a great deal of time trying to cover the sound with my TV, hoping a bullet would not come through the wall. When I would see her in passing on the sidewalk, she would never make eye contact. When I'd ask her how things were, she'd say they were good. Oh, how I remembered those days of denial.

What I didn't recognize at the time was that I was sinking. I was merging myself into my neighbor's situation. I was becoming the victim along with her, and in my mind, experiencing the violence with her. I sought to stay away from home as much as possible and would drive in circles around the parking lot looking for his car. When I didn't see it, I would scurry to my door, run inside, and lock it as quickly as I could.

One evening after a particularly loud fight, the police arrived. I could hear everything outside my front door because my ear was glued to the backside of it, listening for what was happening next door. I was obsessed. The police escorted the young lady and children out and took them away. All the while, her boyfriend was saying, ever so calmly, how much she tended to exaggerate. Not ten minutes later, I heard him with a power drill changing the deadbolt on the front door. When she returned several hours later with the police, she was unable to get in.

I became paralyzed. I didn't open my curtains, eat, or leave my apartment, not even to go to work. I lost all track of time. I have no idea how long I was like that, lying on my bed with the covers pulled over my head. At one point, I found myself naked, curled up in the bottom of my shower with the water running, crying. After perhaps a week or so, work became concerned about my absences.

Although I was still seeing a therapist I really liked who helped me a lot, I couldn't initially disclose what was going on. I didn't tell him about this in detail. (Note to self: If you don't tell the professional all the information, they can't help you sort it out. It's just like looking for something in the bottom of your purse. Sometimes you just need to dump that thing on the table to see what's in there.)

It is unclear to me if I called my AA sponsor or if she called me. In either case, I am still surprised I was able to get on the phone. Her soft, slow voice was in great contrast to the hysteria going on in my mind, body, and spirit. It was she who walked me, ever so slowly, out of this frenzied condition. I can still hear her gentle voice on the phone with me, "Ah, sweetie, let's just talk for a minute. At this moment, are you alone? (Pause.) Good, honey, just breathe. I won't leave you. I will stay right here on the phone. (Pause.) Is anyone harming you right now? No? (Pause.) Good, just breathe. You're doing great. Breathe. I am right here with you. It's just you and me. Breathe. At this moment, are you okay?"

I would learn that what I had experienced was post-traumatic stress disorder (PTSD). My mind had been catapulted back in time by the similar traumatic circumstances I was exposed to over an extended number of days. In my mind, I was actively suffering abuse all over again, and it felt very, very real.

After finally disclosing all of this to my therapist, he helped me understand I hadn't healed from my time with my abuser. I had been rescued. I had left my relationship with Curtis by immediately entering another relationship. I had gone from a man harming me to a man protecting me and had never dealt with the emotions and thought processes that accompanied leaving the violent situation. I had never learned to be alone. I was forty-four years old and had never lived alone. I had gone from my mother's home to friends' houses, to Job Corps, to Curtis, and then immediately to Mark. There had never been any time of self-reliance or God-reliance. I had to go through the process, not around it. I also needed to move.

I am happy to say the Lord has now healed me emotionally from that traumatic experience. But I will never forget how devastating it was. I learned very well that if issues are not dealt with, they do not go away. I clearly understood I had the capacity for another PTSD episode. I feared the experience of entering a memory I couldn't get out of. Memories can affect you in many ways—some of which you may never even recognize. I feel very strongly that a therapist can be helpful to everyone. Everyone needs a safe place to let their secrets out and know they are still acceptable. My advice is if you are going to spend your time and money working with a therapist, share your entire self with them. Otherwise, by my example, what's the point?

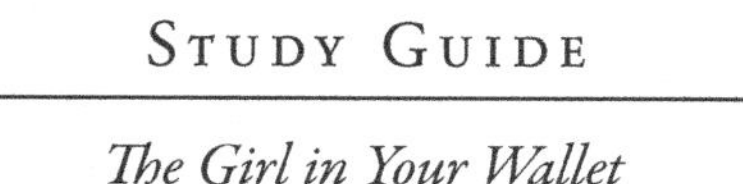

Study Guide

The Girl in Your Wallet

Chapter 17: Releasing the Power of Your Past

What is your initial reaction to the "crab in the bucket" story? Do you agree or disagree? Why or why not?

Have you ever found yourself or witnessed someone else merging into another person's reality as if it were your/their own? In what circumstances?

Immediately following this PTSD episode, I wanted to blame my therapist. Thankfully, I also had my sponsor's counsel to balance my thoughts. Do you have more than one advisor?

Have you ever seen a counselor/therapist and then filtered what information you shared with them? What drove you to do this?

CHAPTER 18

Victim or Volunteer?

"May your choices reflect your hopes, not your fears."
—Nelson Mandela

AFTER MY DIVORCE from Mark, I went looking for family for comfort, which means I went looking for something I needed from someone who was unable to provide it. Again. What transpired between this family member and me was very sad but revealing. After reminding me about what a bad mother I was and itemizing the things I had to do to fix my life, he ranted about how stupid I was and criticized me for my failings. Tears finally streamed down my face, but I remained silent. I didn't accept any of the things he was hurling at me. I had healed beyond these tactics. My foundation and forgiveness were intact. I wept because deep in my heart, I knew this relationship was so badly damaged that I could no longer be around him. At all.

It's not always about what happens, but about what happens next. After he left, I had a good cry and then dialed my friend Leslie's phone number and told her what had happened. She quietly listened while I carried on, trying to purge every detail and get them out of me. After I calmed down and began to have brief lapses in speech, she spoke. She told me she was sorry I'd had this experience. Then she very calmly asked me how much power I was going to give him and how long I was going to let it bother me. She helped me to see that, yet again, no one could steal my peace without my permission. If I had stopped to think about it, I could have seen I was looking for trouble. Was I a victim or a volunteer?

I am not strong enough to pull my family out of their strongholds and belief systems. Nor is it my job. They are, however, strong enough to pull me in. I wish this weren't the case, but I have to limit my exposure because that comfortable dysfunction has a lure. In much the same way that it's a bad idea for an alcoholic to hang out at a bar, if I spend too much time with my family-of-origin, their way of thinking begins to make sense. I love them dearly, but I need to do it from a distance.

I waited years for the past to change, not recognizing that was what I was doing. I also realized my past had become an idol for me in a very distorted way. I pondered it often. I allowed my perceptions to alter my decisions and alienate me from healthy, encouraging people. I had also used the anger it held as the drive to keep going some days. I carried that heavily chained legacy of my past, dragging it behind me like a dead body for years, and I had been exhausted by it. Would I pick it up again because of one bad encounter? An encounter I had invited? I was no longer full of shame and regret, yet it was available to me should I decide to take the bait. It is always there, lying in wait for me. Today, I choose not to take the bait.

But How Can You Tell?

I've learned to listen for the progression of a potential dysfunctional relationship. It can start innocently enough but eventually leads to control and belittling. Each statement below shows how such a progression can happen.

1. "Do you need help with that?"

2. "Here, let me do that for you."

3. "You know you can't do that without me. Just let me do it."

4. "Why do you even try?"

5. "You can't do anything without me, and you know it."

In a recent visit to my hometown and an old friend's home, I had the uncomfortable opportunity to observe the same dysfunction I'd experienced early in my life. I witnessed my friend ranting on at least six different occasions. He stood over his girlfriend, arms flailing, voice raised, shouting, "She (his girlfriend) would never have made it without me! She'd be dead right now! Her family is so bad that she would never have made it if I hadn't come along. She needs me, and she knows it! She's lucky I found her when I did!"

Trying to have a conversation with her, I'd ask her a question. My friend would answer for her. As she drew in a breath to speak, he overpowered her verbally. It was a valuable reminder of how I had been taught to believe in a woman's inferiority and lack of value.

> Jim—(speaking to my mom): "Your kids are just lucky I came along when I did. You were never going to make it without me."
>
> Curtis—Reminding me I was never going to amount to anything, that I needed him to survive, that the only guy who would ever want me was a drunk in a bar. "I can't believe how stupid you are. Why can't you just stand there and look good?" (You don't need to speak; your words/thoughts have no value.)

> Mark—"Wow, you can't remember anything, can you? It's a good thing I'm here. Don't worry about it. I'll take care of it. We both know I will do it right."

That message of worthlessness was deeply ingrained in me over decades, and long after my abusers left my life, I continued their work, restating that message over-and-over again. In my childhood, I had no control. Later, I believe I not only allowed this kind of negative talk to be directed at me, but there's also a very good chance that I drew it to me. It was easier to believe the bad stuff. Controlling men seem to have an eye for spotting behaviors that will allow or invite their dominance in a relationship. Now I understand I have a choice. As I left my friends' house that day, my heart was deeply saddened. I pray for them both and know that is where my influence ends.

The progression is usually very subtle, but in my experience, such men are paying close attention to whether you have boundaries, whether you will accept or even notice when the language changes. You are auditioning in a way. He wants you to be completely dependent on him. I believe that while women are confused and hurt when a man doesn't want to be in a relationship with them, it may very well be that he didn't see you as a viable victim. Consider that the next time you're feeling sorry for yourself in that moment of loneliness. You may need to turn that into gratefulness. You may have just escaped a whole lot of trouble.

Bad Boys, What's the Attraction?

Who knows? Perhaps it is just our sinful nature to want to live with an edge of danger in our lives. What I know for sure is I somehow believed I could control the amount of "bad" in the boy. I wanted them to bring it out and put it away based on how I felt at any given moment, but it doesn't work that way. Maybe this falls into the same category as "he just hasn't met the right girl yet" and "I'm the one he would change for." When those negative qualities remained or escalated, I was somehow offended, almost like I had been deceived. No, I had all the information. The deception was that I chose not to believe it. Hmm...victim or volunteer?

I am no longer looking for a Savior. I have found Him. He had been there all along. These dark times solidified that my first and foremost relationship is with God. Every other relationship is secondary and must be. It is only because He first loved me, and I accepted it that I could show love to anyone else. The love I expressed prior was one of self-centeredness and reliance on another. I am good enough, I am smart enough, and God would not bring me this far without giving me the power and wisdom I need. The key to this is asking Jesus daily for that power and wisdom. I was right to realize I did not have it on my own. The lie was that I would find it in another human being.

Loser Magnet

Many of us have seen the Cinderella-style movie *Pretty Woman*. There is a tender moment when Julia Roberts's character, a free-spirited hooker-for-hire, discloses to her knight in shining armor (Richard Gere) that her mother calls her a "Loser Magnet." Looking back, I know I attracted "losers" because of what I believed about myself. As a result, I only considered men who were within my class of life. That included ex-cons, future convicts, welfare recipients, violent men. You get the idea. This was the pool I was swimming in. What else did I expect to find? Let's be honest. I wasn't exactly a catch in those days. I totally get this and feel that some of you, if you have read this far, can likely relate to it too. I used to say I could walk into a room, and it was always the abusive guy, the one who had been to prison, tatted up, wearing a wife-beater T-shirt and cocky smile, who was the one I found attractive.

I see now how thinking I was a "loser magnet" became a self-fulfilling prophecy. What I believe today is that all those "losers" I was attracted to were profiling me. I was an easy target for a predator. I can now see I was an eager participant in the selection of my abusers. My shoulders were slumped down, and my eyes faced down, unable to make eye contact for more than a second. My body language spoke volumes. As the places I frequented changed, so did my behavior.

In 2015, I attended a volunteer training seminar at a non-profit started by a police officer who worked nights in an area known for prostitution. It broke his heart arresting these women over-and-over again. At the training, we learned the harsh truth about the daily existence of these young women and the lies they believe that cause them to go back to jail repeatedly:

1. They almost always come from fatherless homes.

2. Many have not experienced healthy, loving parental love from a trustworthy male in their lives.

3. This drive is so strong that many pimps further capitalize by requiring their working girls to call them "Daddy."

Most shocking to me was how these women are being recruited. Young girls, ages 12-18, tend to travel in packs to familiar places like the mall, bowling alley, movies, etc. There are young men, who are also recruited for their looks and charm, sent out to search for vulnerable girls. A group of young girls is all laughs and giggles. The predator's target is the one who is trailing behind and exhibiting submissive body language: slumped shoulders, head tilted down, wringing hands. She may be walking three feet behind the group, her clothes aren't quite as current, and she likely has trouble making eye contact. In a group of her peers, she is likely in the shadow of the other girls. She is the one.

He walks past the cheerleader types and other popular girls and turns his attention directly at her. He makes eye contact, makes her feel important. He may bring her gifts, call her often, and listen to her when she speaks. She falls dreamily in love with him, and he begins to isolate her from her friends. After all, shouldn't he be enough for her? Doesn't she love him? Then he asks her to do a favor for him, just this one time.

Let me tie this all together. I have two pictures of myself from my junior high school. In one, I'm smiling brightly, chin up, looking at the camera. The other is from the following year. My head is tilted down, and I am barely making eye contact with the photographer. My shoulders are slumped. The difference between these two pictures is shame, embarrassment, guilt. Bad things happened in the year between those photos. Men who dominate or mean harm are looking for these qualities in women, and we are easy prey. This training really opened my eyes.

Identifying Your Distractions

We may find some men appealing because they trigger familiar dysfunctional behavior in us. Satan will use whatever tactic works to steer us off course. I have heard it said he doesn't have to be very creative because we fall for the same things repeatedly. I would have to agree.

One example of this for me happened when I went to an AC/DC concert alone. It wasn't my first time going to a show by myself. I had learned to do many things alone. The man in the seat next to me arrived, and to say he was intoxicated would be a huge understatement. His eyes were rolled back in his head, and his arms were flailing about to the music. This guy was wasted. I was doing my best to keep my distance while staying near my seat when a guy from about four seats away walked over and offered me the seat next to him. He suggested I would be safer, and I agreed. (Can you say rescued?)

It turns out Richard and his friend were visiting from Oregon.

I enjoyed having someone to chat and joke with as I watched the concert. He had a great sense of humor. The banter was easy, and at the end of the night, he asked for my number, and I gave it to him. Very soon after, as I was getting on the train home, I received my first text from him, telling me he'd had fun. Me too, I replied. I must have received ten texts and three phone calls in the next twenty-four hours, and they did not stop. I found the attention irresistible.

The more Richard texted, the more I found myself on the edge of my seat with anticipation. He shared many of the same characteristics as both my first husband and the guys from the old neighborhood where I grew up. He was street smart, sarcastic, demeaning to women, vulgar, and likely an alcoholic. It triggered a level of comfort in me that I should have found alarming. In hindsight, I know God was warning me to get away, but I simply could not resist the attention. A guy showed me some attention and had a sense of humor, and I became addicted to that little notification on my phone. This was not a romantic relationship. We did not hold hands or make out. He was clearly interested in me, and even more so when he learned I owned my own business. The texts and phone calls were continuous, and he even drove up from the Portland area to visit me on two separate occasions.

Both times, I was uncomfortable and nervous, but I did it anyway. I had no business having this strange man in my house, but I had not laughed in a long time, and he tapped into a long-neglected part of me, the part that liked to play. I was spiraling emotionally and did not even try to consult the Lord regarding His desire for me.

Was this a relapse? Not really. I had never dealt with this before. Richard was also serving a purpose, helping me find the backbone I needed to deal with my newly ex-husband. As Mark and I were still working out some of our split details, Richard gave me a male perspective to consider, which proved to be of great value to me.

I can now see that Richard was testing me every step of the way.

First, it was his crass humor, dirty jokes, and his demeaning comments about women. How would I respond? Well, we all know by now this kind of behavior by men had been my norm, so very little shocked me, and I laughed it off. He moved on to forwarding me dirty joke texts that he and his friends circulated, some of them mildly pornographic. Again, I laughed it off, maybe making some comments about his low opinion of women, but not really drawing a line in the sand, just suggesting that it was in poor taste. He had many stories about the dating escapades his friends had experienced, all in bad taste and vivid detail. Are you getting the idea here? He was testing me to see what I would tolerate, where my threshold was. And I drew no line. My efforts to be fun and agreeable showed him that I had no boundaries and that all of it was permissible.

It is mind-boggling to think I could revert that far back so quickly, but I most certainly did. I had so much anxiety all the time that I had difficulty eating. My stomach was quivering. This was a reaction I had never had before in my life, stress always triggered appetite, but this was not stress. I was actively going against my God-given radar, the internal warning system that keeps me in God's will or, at the very least, keeps me out of danger. I cannot even claim I didn't know this, and however bizarre it may sound, after years of neglect and isolation, I was starving for affection. This was willful disobedience.

The pinnacle of my madness was when I found myself standing in the liquor store purchasing a half-gallon of vodka for his upcoming two-day visit. I was a recovering alcoholic, seventeen years sober, sixteen years a Christian, standing in line at the liquor store to buy booze for a man I didn't even like. It amazes me how I could have been so needy that I let any shred of confidence and emotional stability I'd built get pulled out from under me like a throw rug. Of course, I shared these details with no other person, friend, or therapist. I carefully tailored the information to sound like we were just having fun and I could take it or leave it when the reality was if he didn't call or text me, often I would find some reason to reach out to him.

I am grateful for a friend who, at a gathering, leaned over my chair, looked me in the eye, and asked rather loudly, "Who are you?" She persisted in asking me more and more questions. I appreciate her courage in asking me if this was the vision I had for the next chapter of my life. Next chapter? She was suggesting I could shape my future, that I had a choice. I had to face that I was traveling down a familiar road that would take me back to where I had already been. I remembered being in those horrible dysfunctional and painful relationships, and I was headed there again, by my own choice! I wasn't a victim. I was a volunteer.

Breaking off my relationship with Richard was a challenge, but I did it. Gratefully, this period didn't last very long because I was able to come to my senses. I never want to forget that it happened.

I have two big takeaways from this entire experience. First, God must always be my number one priority. Whenever I place anyone else in that position, I am doomed to failure and defeat.

"Thou shalt have no other gods before me."

—Exodus 20:3 (KJV)

The second thing I know for sure is that a guy is on his best behavior at the beginning of a relationship. No, Richard and I weren't dating, but the principle still stands. It will not get any better than that. If you put up with any unacceptable behaviors, you can only expect them to increase over time as he relaxes around you. He is trying to impress you, to win you over! Whatever you tolerate is what you can expect to get more of.

Every time I hear a woman talk about the guy she is dating as "having potential," I want to scream. He is exactly who you see, and no human force can change him. You are not that powerful. Sorry. Mark told me early on I would never be his number-one priority, but

I dismissed it. Enormous mistake. It never changed. God alone can change a person, and if he's the right guy for you, why would he need to change, anyway? Please stop with the fairy-tale thinking that "he just hasn't met the right girl yet to settle down." And please stop telling your daughters this fallacy! This is just something Hollywood screenwriters write about, and pop singers sing about. With all due respect to the stars of our day, their message is not the real world.

Tearing myself away from this dysfunction and constant attention from Richard was a different story, however. Let's not forget how very lonely I was. I made a list of things I didn't like about him: he dominates the conversation, always talks about himself, he's an alcoholic, he makes you feel bad about yourself. I wrote these things on a three-by-five index card and used a rubber band to secure it around my phone. I could not answer my phone or read a text without seeing my list. This was a huge help.

I also changed my ringtone and text alert sounds. I was programmed just like Pavlov's dog; I heard that familiar sound, and I went running for attention. Sometimes I still hear that standard T-Mobile text alert sound on someone else's phone while I'm in a grocery store, and I smile and praise my Father in heaven for deliverance.

I only heard from Richard one more time, well over a year later. He called me at work and asked how I was, to which I replied, good. He said he and his son were coming up to Seattle, and he wanted to have lunch. I told him I would be at church for a marriage event with my boyfriend. I never heard from him again.

In my time of great weakness and vulnerability, Richard showed up, providing the attention and laughter I had not had in a long time. It tapped into that old me, the insecure little girl who still believed this was how a man behaves, and that crass humor was funny. I would have never guessed I'd still be attracted to that old pattern, having been delivered from so many areas of bondage. But, as I can testify, I most certainly was.

Chapter 18: Victim or Volunteer?

What did Leslie do first before she gently confronted me about my response to my family member?

___

___

___

Do you have a "Leslie" in your life? If so, let's honor them by writing their name here. ______________ If not, we will have suggestions a little later.

The messages a child hears growing up become the self-talk and belief of the adult. How does this help explain why women seem to "invite" or draw to themselves the very thing they say they don't want?

___

___

___

Were you surprised at the subtle progression in the language of controlling men? How have you witnessed this in your life or in someone close to you?

___

___

___

When I choose to ignore or deny the behaviors in a potential romantic relationship, what lie (fallacy) am I telling myself?

Negative self-talk turns into negative beliefs, which turns into corresponding behaviors. Those behaviors brought me into a high likelihood of meeting the same type of guy again and again. How can you relate?

I share my experience at volunteer training for a non-profit. Was any part of it a surprise to you?

Have you ever considered you are being evaluated for compliance by a dominating personality? Do you think this happens in platonic relationships as well? Explain.

I was having both a negative emotional and physical response to Richard. Have you ever felt swept away in a new relationship, platonic or romantic, and overlooked the warnings? What qualities did you overlook? How did the relationship work out?

____

____

____

I hadn't had fun for a long time, so when a new person showed up, it derailed my progress. Complete the following sentence for yourself.

> "I haven't enjoyed ________________ for a long time." (There may be more than one.)
>
> This may be your place of weakness. If you are attempting to overcome areas in your life, this may be the entry point for outside influences to hold you back.

What were some of the tangible steps I took to tear myself away from Richard's dysfunction and attention? List at least three.

1. ____
2. ____
3. ____
4. ____
5. ____

a. How can you adopt these actions to move away from an undesirable situation/person?

____

____

____

b. Did the language you used in your answer above leave an opening to revisit the situation or did it reflect permanence? Journal your thoughts here.

____

____

____

c. In my example with Richard, I made a permanent decision in an instant. Some relationships will require slowly moving away. Remember, every decision doesn't require a declaration. You needn't make an announcement to take action.

CHAPTER 19

Trying Something New

"Men respect standards. Get some."

—Steve Harvey, *Act Like a Lady, Think Like a Man*

A YEAR OR so after the Richard fiasco, my therapist suggested I start dating. I was against it, but I heard him out. Since I had never dated in the traditional sense, he thought it might be wise to get familiar with the process and not practice on someone I truly liked. The fact that I was forty-four and had never been on a date or had a boyfriend caused me apprehension. I was reaching a point where my thinking was shifting. I had endured so many painful and terrifying things in my life that had produced no good results. I was becoming willing to endure some discomfort for some new, potentially positive experiences. His suggestion made sense to me and, after consulting my sponsor, I agreed to give it a try. I went, we ate, and it was done. My starter date was completed.

Ironically, some of the best dating advice I got was from my son, who was then in his late twenties. He told me two things:

1. Date someone for at least three months before deciding you know who they are. Anyone can keep up an act for that long.

2. Ask his friends about him.

I agreed the first one was good advice, but I challenged the second suggestion. I said the guy's friends would cover for him. He came back firmly and said, "If you ask his friends and he is really a jerk, they will go quiet on you. They won't trash their buddy, even if it's true. If they tell you he is a great guy, it's because he is."

Words of wisdom from my offspring.

Outside My Comfort Zone

I can think of a couple of things that changed my social trajectory. Both were life-changing, although one might seem rather silly. I watched the Jim Carrey movie *Yes, Man*. Then I watched it again. Then three times in one month. Was it Oscar-worthy? No. But there was a principle in it I was open to learning. I was recognizing that my language and mannerisms were likely keeping people at a distance. As much as I craved interaction with people, my instinctive reaction was to say no to an invitation and then reconsider it later. The unpleasant side effect of this is that people generally stop asking you when you say no too often. They assume your answer already.

With this newfound awareness, I began to accept invitations quickly. Then I ran into another problem. I was standing in my kitchen at a dinner event when I told someone, "Sounds fun. Let's do it." That was when my friend Kathy commented, "Don't hold your breath. She has about a 40 percent follow-through rate." Ouch! That hurt. She was right. I had gone from one extreme to the other. I would accept the invitation on the spot and then cancel later when I had considered it or checked my schedule. Still, I was making progress.

Another thing that happened was over lunch with a business associate. She suggested I explore Meetup.com. I had no idea what it was, but I needed some people in my life. I perused the website and saw some groups on the homepage that I wasn't interested in, so I stopped looking. When I saw her and again mentioned I needed some activities and new people in my life, she gave me a tutorial, and I went back onto the website.

Shifting Perspective

I used to say that Meetup changed my life, which is somewhat accurate. What I see now is that the more I became willing to open myself up to new ideas, the more opportunities I recognized. It turns out there was a whole world I had yet to learn how to participate in. I cautiously created my profile and joined several groups. I watched the activity in these groups for a month or so before I attended an event. I went to hiking, social, and dinner events. I wasn't looking for a mate when Scott and I met, although we were at a singles event. I was simply following the suggestion in Dr. Henry Cloud's book *How to Get a Date Worth Keeping*. As I recall, the premise was to stop looking for a husband and get out and meet some people. So that's what I did.

A game night was posted on a Meetup.com singles group. Since I had been to several different meetups, it was no longer that intimidating to walk into a group of strangers. Approximately seventy-five people were at game tables spread throughout the large house and yard. I happened to sit at *Mexican Train* with six or so other people, which included Scott, who was sitting across the table. I was playful and silly; it was a game night, after all. After that game ended, we took a short break, and I moved to another table and sat next to Scott. We packed in around the folding table and played the game. When it was over, Scott and I engaged in some conversation, which felt comfortable. I didn't see him as a threat. We went our separate ways and mingled with the other guests.

Scott caught my attention for several reasons:

1. I was relaxed around him.

2. He had tattoos, so he wasn't likely to judge me for mine.

3. He had a job.

4. His only daughter was grown.

5. He could take a joke, which I learned at the game tables.

When it came time to leave, I sought Scott out and told him I had enjoyed meeting him. He walked with me to the door and asked if I would like to get lunch sometime. Sure. I gave him my number. He gave me his business card. There were no fireworks, no racing thoughts about what I should have said, or overanalyzing what I did say. No wishing I had worn different clothes. I had determined I would be who I was no matter where I was or who I was with. I was done pretending. I wasn't sure if he would call or not, and I didn't sit by the phone waiting. I pinned his business card on my bulletin board and moved on.

A few days later, Scott called. Would I like to meet him for lunch on Wednesday? I said, "Yes, that would be nice." I have often replayed walking into that restaurant and making eye contact with that handsome man as he rose from his seat in the lobby. We had a nice lunch and conversation, and he walked me to my car. Two days later, I received a second call with a second invitation to lunch. Would I like to choose the restaurant this time? Sure. Scott attended both of our lunch "dates," wearing his work clothes of slacks and a button-down shirt. This caused me a bit of a pause. I was not accustomed to a world where men dressed professionally, particularly for lunch.

Our first official date, an evening meal, came several weeks later. Honestly, I was astonished he was still interested in me. I thought the world of this man. He had served twenty years in the United States

Air Force, had an MBA, and was now working in a high-level position in the federal government. I had been transparent to a certain degree, not disclosing my entire life story, yet he still wanted to spend time with me. He was highly intelligent and very analytical. Surely, he could see my defects, right? These were the same tired tapes from days of old popping up, and while at some level I thought he would wise up about me soon, there was another presence in my spirit. This presence was gentle, quieter, and it simply observed. I didn't react. I was calm as I considered this emerging relationship. The presence in my spirit told me not to run, either into it or from it, and to let it play out in its own time. It didn't require my obsessive focus.

I accepted Scott's invitation to dinner and gave him my address. He arrived five minutes early, walked me to the car, and opened my car door for me. We had learned we had similar taste in music during our earlier conversations, so he had some samples of things he was enjoying ready to play for our drive. We had a reservation at a very nice waterfront seafood restaurant. I ordered the garlic shrimp, and he did too, commenting to the server that he should probably eat garlic as well since he might want to kiss me later. This made me smile. He reviewed the wine list and asked if I would like a glass. I used the opportunity to tell him I did not drink. Ever? No, not ever. I watched his reaction carefully. In my experience, those who place a great deal of value on their drinking will want to know why you don't drink or encourage you to drink. He simply asked if it would bother me if he had a glass. No, please do.

The reason I include all of this isn't because it was a special meal spent with an attractive man. I was learning. He arrived early. This was important. It meant I had value. He treated me well by opening the car and restaurant doors for me. This showed respect. He took me to a seafood restaurant because I liked seafood. He has an incredibly strong gag reflex to fish, although I didn't know it at the time. It was important to me, so it was important to him. He even struggled to eat that shrimp. I also learned he might kiss me later. It had been years and turned out to be worth the wait.

With his arm resting on the small of my back, he led me from the restaurant to the car. As we were pulling out of the parking space, I spoke up. "Could we pull back in for a minute?" He looked confused but complied. Then I said something I never thought I could or would. I asked, "How about we just have that kiss now?"

He was a bit surprised, but he smiled and complied with my request. I wanted something, and I spoke the words out loud. I took the risk. I owned my space. I was empowered. We sat in that car, with the motor running, I might add, for hours, talking, holding hands, and smooching. In our peripheral vision, we noticed dinner patrons coming and going and that the sun had gone down. We eventually left the restaurant, and he drove me home. At the door, he told me he would have eventually gotten around to that kiss, but I had saved him a lot of time. He let me know he was enjoying getting to know me, but he was not a young man driven by hormones anymore. He would not enter into a sexual relationship with a woman again until he knew there was compatibility and a shot at something real. Imagine that—one evening filled with two adults speaking their truths out loud to each other. I had nothing but respect for this man and still do. This early experience has led to years of open communication. If you have never had it, I wish this for you. It took courage, and it was worth it.

I could tell you many special things my husband did early on and continues to do that caused me to fall in love with him even more. I could tell you about the romantic dates and special gifts. Those would all be true. He swept me off my feet. In keeping with my purpose here, though, I will continue to answer how I knew he was a good man and not like the others.

My husband, Scott, is extremely supportive, and I know for sure he is a gift from God. He is a man of his convictions, is not easily manipulated, and encourages me to be all God wants me to be, not what he wants me to be. I am blessed daily.

So, how did I know that Scott was a good choice for me? I didn't. I had just finished reading Steve Harvey's book *Act Like a Lady, Think Like a Man*. I was in my mid-forties, twice divorced, had two older brothers, and had grown up surrounded by their male friends. If the information in this book was correct, I knew very little about men. I had written in the margins of the book, documenting the mistakes and warning signs I had made or overlooked. Steve was describing them plain as day. I asked a guy friend about a couple of things in the book, and he looked at me like I was ridiculous. "Of course, that's how we think; you know that." Nope, I really didn't, and neither did my girlfriends. I could finally see the reality was there the whole time. Buy the book. You won't be sorry.

These were my observations:

1. Scott has always made me feel important. From the first motorcycle ride he took me on, he has referred to me as "precious cargo."

2. He showed up when he said he was going to show up.

3. I was important to him, and it showed. The day he introduced me as his girlfriend, I was overwhelmed with joy. He said, "This is my girlfriend, Teresa." I don't remember anything he said after that. I'm sure I must have nodded and shaken a hand or something. Steve Harvey says if a man loves you, he will introduce you as the woman he is with and let all the other men in the room know you are off-limits.

4. He would talk about the future, and I was in it.

5. He responded calmly to problems that needed to be solved.

6. I watched his reactions. When he realized his car had a flat tire, he said, "Looks like I am going to have to get my tire changed." No screaming. No blaming. He went right back to what he was talking about before.

7. He noticed how startled I got when he came into a room if I didn't hear him coming. He took it upon himself to begin speaking from far off so I would hear him coming. I made sure he knew how much that meant to me.

8. We can disagree without getting into a heated conversation. We come from two very different backgrounds, and we accept each other for exactly who we are. Since we share similar values, we have fewer major items that we disagree about.

9. I was attending a women's Bible study at my church, and he signed up for the men's group on the same evening unprompted.

10. He didn't hide his phone from me or close his computer windows when I walked into the room. (Somebody needs to hear this!)

11. When he received money from his mother's estate, he bought me a car, and he has never mentioned it again.

I am colorful, and Scott is literal. I tell a good story. He tells an accurate story. Scott is consistent and regimented, and I find that incredibly attractive, along with his silver hair. He can change course if he wants to, but he doesn't leave the house without a destination. To me, a destination can be "north." For a girl who has lacked structure her entire life, I sink down into his calmness like a warm blanket and slowly exhale. Very early on, when I told him how much this meant to me, he said that some women might find that quality boring. I assured him only the wrong woman would. I am all-in.

Is our relationship perfect? Not a chance. I know who he is, and he is the same guy day after day, no matter where we are or whom we're with. His insides match his outsides. I can list the habits or qualities I can do without, but what's the point? I determined a long time ago that if we are solid on the main things, the rest of that stuff is just stuff. We understand and agree on God's design. We love God first, family second, and others third. He doesn't need rescuing. Neither do I.

When choosing a relationship, the question becomes whether you want to hitch your wagon to that man knowing he has a porn addiction, drinks too much, makes jokes at your expense, doesn't parent the children from his last marriage, or raises a hand to you. The list goes on and on. Remember, he is on his best behavior when you are dating. He will only relax from there. If he can't be on time now, you shouldn't expect that to get any better.

Do Scott and I argue? Rarely. We disagree often, but it isn't that big of a deal. When the big stuff is lined up, there is less to bicker over. Age also helps. We both had bad relationships in our pasts that we choose to learn from regarding what doesn't work. We occasionally bump heads. Recently, he said how much he appreciated me not coming at him full throttle like I used to. I snickered inwardly. He has never seen full throttle. I am not that girl anymore, and this pleases me.

I do not disrespect my husband to anyone. Nor will I be in the presence of anyone who disrespects him. It may sound like we don't joke around, but that couldn't be further from the truth. I missed out on my first childhood, so I play around like a five-year-old a lot in the privacy of our own home.

One of the sweetest things I share with Scott is bedtime prayer. I don't remember the subject on one specific night, but lying on our pillows face-to-face, I asked, "What do you think is going to happen?" He was quiet for a short moment and softly said, "I think some stuff is going to happen, then some other stuff, and then we will die and go be with Jesus." It's amazing what happened when I got out of the way and allowed God to select my spouse. Yep, just like being wrapped in a warm blanket.

Study Guide

The Girl in Your Wallet

Chapter 19: Trying Something New

In my opinion, what is the premise in Dr. Henry Cloud's *How to Get a Date Worth Keeping?*

Often, we seek out information to support what we already believe. My openness to learn something new led me to Steve Harvey's *Act Like a Lady, Think Like a Man.* How willing are you to consider and implement new (and likely uncomfortable) ideas for personal growth?

How do your actions correspond with your answer above? State a specific example of when you sought out new information and implemented it into your life.

What became the basis, the foundation, of my relationship with Scott that eliminated most conflict?

A man who was not easily manipulated was my best choice since it had been my standard operating procedure early in my life. Manipulation implies I know what is best, and others should follow my ideas. Up to this point in my life, is there evidence that I had known what was best for me?

I do not always need to be right, but I do need to be heard. How much time do you spend trying to convince others you are right when you ultimately want to be heard and understood?

Think about social media. Are you obsessively posting opinion pieces? If so, what is driving that behavior?

SECTION THREE

Where I Am Now
Healing the Broken Places

Healing has been a journey, and as I said, the work continues. Today, through my faith and working with my sponsor and counselors, I have a level of peace and self-acceptance. Forgiveness has been key—forgiveness for myself, and forgiveness for others. I had a "right" to be angry about the hurtful things that had been done to me, but that right" kept me, not others, in bondage. Ruminating on the mistreatment to me resulted in the same thing every time. I was left resentful, wallowing in self-pity, and reliving the emotions that accompanied the act itself. I imagined that if the other person would admit their wrongs and apologize, I would be released from my inner turmoil, that it could somehow be "undone." It had been decades, and no one had come to do that. I was the only one suffering.

CHAPTER 20

Mining the Ruins

"Then you will know the truth, and the truth will set you free."
—John 8:32 NIV

NOW THAT I have some distance from the events that happened with my stepfather Jim, and I have an adult mindset to consider them, I believe his initial intention with our family was honorable. He would not have taken a woman with two children into his life and helped us out of a devastating domestic violence situation without having some intention of doing right by our family. So, I must believe his intentions were good. I don't know much about his history, but he was a Vietnam veteran. I remember at a very young age seeing him in full dress uniform. He was my dad's best friend, and to the best of my memory, he was always around. I guess that's how he and my mother got to know each other so well. As I've said before, my dad was a violent drunk, and Jim most certainly witnessed my mother's beatings. I know he had two children who still lived in California whose pictures he carried around with him, although he hadn't spoken to them in many, many years.

The truth is I don't think I was ever truly as angry with Jim as I was with my mother. The real fact is I don't think I've ever been as mad at men as I have been with women. I grew up in an environment that raised men to a higher level of importance. Women were there to serve as entertainment and, essentially, as servants. The women in the groups I grew up with viewed each other as competition. I don't remember any of the women ever sticking around for too long. I assume they were either party girls, or they wised up and moved on. I love that the Lord has created such a heart in me for women and now calls me to minister to them.

Although I may not have been as angry with Jim, I was certainly repulsed by him. Every time I went back to visit my mother, I could feel his eyes scanning me. I just felt dirty and helpless. Whenever I was in his presence, my emotional condition returned to the same state I had been in when I lived there. So how do I forgive a man who so badly damaged me emotionally and sexually, who violated my self-worth, and who further embedded the negative belief that my mother planted in my thinking about only being valuable in service to men?

How did I forgive Jim, and in doing so, forgive Curtis?

1. I understood God wanted me to. God loved them too.

2. I wanted to. I had been walking with the Lord long enough and been set free from so much. I wanted out from under this. It was heavy, and I was tired.

3. I was able to forgive them because by working through the Twelve Steps and going to counseling, I became more aware of the people I'd harmed. I'd done devastating things and could no longer hold others to a standard I could not achieve. My sins were different but no less harmful to others.

Another incident served as an illustration of how things can get out of control. It began in 2001 when I had to undergo serious back surgery. I had had one procedure already and believed I had been "fixed." They told me to limit the amount of weight I was lifting going forward, but sadly, I did not follow their advice. It wasn't long before I was back in surgery, having two vertebrae in my lower spine fused. I should have been out of work for three months, but through a series of unforeseen events, it turned into eleven months. So, for eleven months, I was home with nothing to do all day. At first, I was so heavily medicated with painkillers that it didn't make any difference. As I began to come out of the fog, my mind wandered. I started thinking about the good old days, back when I had friends. Dangerously, I started glamorizing the friends I'd been hanging out with just before being arrested and going to jail. My mind began to focus on one of the guys I had developed a closer "friendship" with: Mike S.

Although I knew Mike S. lived in Tacoma, I found no useful information on the Internet. So, I looked up his family name in the state of Michigan. I started dialing the phone and finally stumbled across one family member who gave me another number, and eventually, I spoke to his mother. She relayed the message to Mike S., and within a couple of days, he called me. Three days after that, I met him at a restaurant for lunch. He showed up with a Motel 6 key in his hand. It turns out he had regretted not taking that additional step with me before and assumed I was still willing. It was a big lesson to me that he had that room key. You see, he was sure, based on my interest and effort in getting in touch with him, that it was to close that deal. For him, he was certain we were going to have sex. We did not.

What does all this have to do with me forgiving Jim? I could see firsthand that even as an honest Christian woman, too much idle time and pain medication caused me to put myself in a situation I would have never dreamed possible. There I was, spending my days hunting down an old love interest. While I never followed through on the actual deal, I cannot discount that an idle mind is the devil's workshop. I had thought it through, blazed past multiple obstacles, and found this guy. Satan had hold of me, and I was along for the ride.

I have heard people talk about what the devil stole from them. With me, he didn't need to steal anything. I willingly gave it away. So, I thought back to Jim. His interest in me sexually, his constant comments, his groping me when my mother's back was turned, his list of everything I did wrong so he could enforce punishment—these had all happened during the time after that swimming pool had landed on his back. He was stuck in the house for two years on pain medication. He had nothing but time on his hands, and he didn't even have the benefit of having a relationship with Christ.

Similarly, I had recreated the circumstances that he had experienced. God had given me a glimpse of what it must have been like for him too. Add to that a naïve young woman with low-cut blouses, tight blue jeans, and way too much makeup, and you have a recipe for disaster. I am *not* saying what he did was excusable. What I am saying is: *He that is without sin among you, let him first cast a stone at her. (John 8:7, KJV)*

I promptly dropped the rock I held in my hand. I believe he had recognition and remorse. I could let it go. Big exhale. Just breathe.

Healing from the Unspeakable

Even though I had forgiven Jim and Curtis, there was more to deal with. Getting over the sexual abuse itself would be my most time-consuming issue. I had long since been removed from the situation, but snippets of memories still replayed in my mind randomly. Whether it was provoked by a conversation or who knows what, I would slide into my head and isolate myself. Having gone through the forgiveness steps of letting Jim and Curtis off the hook, the strong, sometimes violent feelings associated with the abuse had been alleviated. What I was left with wasn't necessarily negative. I was conflicted.

I would understand my conflict more fully as a participant in a small group led by a trained psychologist. We had spent several days sharing and creating an environment of trust. I think it helped that we were strangers from all around the country. A brave gentleman shared that he had been sexually abused as a child at the hands of a trusted male adult. As he worked to find words to explain and release these long-stowed feelings and memories, he said he had spent his life wondering if he was gay. He had never said those words out loud before, and it was clearly very difficult for him. (In sharing this, I need to note that we had the guidance of trained psychologists. This is deep-level, emotional stuff, so a trained professional is strongly advised.)

Our facilitator carefully ventured into it in this way—she said the body is wired with many nerve endings that provide us with warning signals. Physical pain lets us know that something is harmful to us, and pleasure is designed to allow us to feel relaxed or excited so we can enjoy it. The physical body does not always correlate with whether the pleasure centers are being activated by an act of abuse or consent. It is designed to respond in a specific way.

She used an example of a cat who puts her paws on your bare skin on your back and kneads, maybe even poking out her claws a bit. Your body responds with a moan, a shiver, or even a warm sensation throughout your back. How much more when the areas of stimulation are sexual? In this illustration, the man was conflicted because his body became aroused by the adult who took advantage of him. He spent the next twenty-five years silently wondering how he could have liked it. Didn't that make him a monster too? He felt like an imposter to his wife and his faith because of this confusion. He carried deep levels of shame inside and shed many tears.

Our leader went on to gently ask him if he was typically attracted to men? Did he seek out a conversation and try to be near a man whom he deemed attractive? No, he wasn't attracted to men, he said. He had no such thoughts or inklings. He was conflicted by his body's betrayal at such a young age, and that experience had tormented him for a lifetime.

I spent the afternoon and evening considering this new information. I could relate to the shame and confusion in my own experience. My conflict lay in my body responding to something so negative and shameful. The experience also played into my inherited value that a woman's worth was defined by her ability to attract a man. Well, I had attracted one, and it was very, very wrong.

I can't tell you how long this process took. Months? Once again, as Light was shined into the dark crevices, that shame lost its hold on me. It stopped being my secret and no longer warranted all the energy it took to hide it and be ashamed of it. I was exhausted. It simply stopped being important to me. When the images appeared in my mind, I was able to observe and not participate emotionally. Over time, they stopped altogether. It also helped me to know I was not alone. I am grateful for this brave soul who felt safe enough to share something so deeply personal with us. I shared in his journey to freedom, and he shared in mine.

As I traveled this healing journey, I also began to understand more about my mother's response to coming face-to-face with my being sexually abused by her husband. I began to have more compassion for her. She not only was losing the security that she had placed entirely in her mate, but she was also losing it to her daughter. I had become the competition. My image of her began to change from resentment to empathy. I was sad for her emptiness.

God has held me close through such deep realizations and healing. I believe our ability to be honest directly correlates to our ability to heal. When I was stuck waiting for my past to change, I avoided facing this experience. It had indeed happened, and no amount of wishing could change it. Once I reached that level of acceptance, I believe God used someone else's experience to reach me when I was ready. Then I could act. Again, I know now that I have been truly healed because I can reflect on the experience without reliving its pain. Images no longer abruptly surface in my mind. I feel no anger, confusion, or shame. I am in a place of observation, not participation. I understand it is over and have had its power over me released. God has brought me full-circle, and I now know peace.

Forgiving the One Who Hurt Me Most

How could I forgive the woman who gave birth to me and then failed to nurture or protect me, was terribly critical of me, and by every indication just wished I wasn't there? How could I forgive the woman who, when I revealed at age fourteen that her husband had been sexually molesting me, then ran from the room telling me to get out of her house, calling me a liar? How could I forgive *that* person?

To give you an idea of how painfully blind my mother was to my deepest feelings, fifteen years after Jim left, she and I were walking through a Walmart when we noticed a pair of boots prominently on display. I made a halfhearted comment about how that boot style always reminded me of Jim because they were the kind he always wore. In return, she said how interesting it was to see him after all those years. "What? You saw him? When?" I asked, stunned. She said, yes, a couple of years ago Jim had come to see her, and she had met with him. He'd come back from California to say he was sorry for the way that he'd handled things. He wanted her to know he regretted it. My entire world went blank at that moment. I lost track of where I was. All sound disappeared, and I asked my mother quietly, "Why didn't you ever tell any of us?" She simply replied, "Why would it matter to any of you?" Then she continued shopping as if nothing had happened.

I was livid. Let's see. Could it have mattered to me because his verbal and sexual abuse resulted in my homelessness and a lifetime of emotional damage?

I had to talk myself out of rage that day. I spent the rest of the afternoon wearing my game face. I manufactured things to talk about, but it took a lot of effort. I remember telling myself, *You can do this, Teresa.*

Asking how I could forgive her is a very good question, one I certainly didn't think I would ever be qualified to answer. I had a rage that consumed me. It was barely concealed just beneath the surface, and every time I saw her, it resurfaced, and I relived it all again and again. I don't know what will work for you. All I know is there was freedom on the other side of my anger, a rage that had consumed me for twenty-plus years. Those are years I will never get back. If you have a similar story, I hope you won't wait as long.

I have already told you my mother was a very critical person. She also lacked the ability to deal with her emotions. When things got tough, she threw things, yelled, and left the room. Then she eventually emerged to clean something obsessively, and we never spoke of it again. It was especially difficult to listen to her criticize other people for their parenting skills. She still does it walking through the mall, making comments about some random mother's shortcomings or over something she saw on TV or read in the newspaper. It is a guaranteed recurring topic, and she has much to say.

One day when she and her husband were visiting, we went out for a drive. She talked about my dad's parents and how horrible they were because, as a young child, my dad would drink the last sips of alcohol in their glasses after a party, and they didn't stop him. She was appalled that they even found it amusing. How disgusting it was to her that this would go on! More astonishing to me is that she couldn't see the similarities between that and the drugs Jim, her husband, gave us when we were preteens. I was twelve when Jim first gave me pot to smoke. As kids, we went out behind the house and sat in a car that didn't run and smoked joints. I remember coming into the house and eating a ton of ice cream and throwing up all over the place while the adults laughed at me. My mother was right there with them. By fourteen, we were drinking alcohol and doing acid (LSD) in our own home. How was this different than my dad finishing the bottles after a party?

There I was, in the car as we drove down I-5 in Seattle, listening to my mom tell us about what horrible parents her in-laws had been. I wanted to scream. The problem was my screaming had never helped. I was stuck in a vicious cycle. I loved her. I hated her. I was her. I remember Mark reaching over and patting my leg, sensing my frustration, and consoling me. He later told me he was sorry and held me while I swung wildly between love and hate: sadness and rage.

I lived with these kinds of emotional swings for decades with my mom. I believed something was going to be different about this visit with my mother or this phone call; this time, she would behave differently. I would rehearse it in my mind. I would say this, and she would say that. When I would see her, and she didn't play her role correctly, I was infuriated. I would idealize a healthy relationship between a mother and daughter and believe we would have that too. Then, when it didn't happen, I was frustrated. She behaved the same way she'd always behaved. She had not given me any indication that she had changed. Any idea I had that she would be the loving mother I saw in Hallmark movies was only in my imagination.

So, Who Was Truly Crazy?

The Bible tells us to honor our father and mother, but it does not limit it to when they deserve it or when I think they deserve it. I struggled as a Christian, wanting to do what God's Word said, but how could I honor *her*? The woman was in denial that any of those past events ever happened, let alone that they would have any lasting negative effect. The most enraging thing she said in any given situation was how her kids had turned out "just fine." I had news for her. We were not "fine." Not a single one of us.

I do not doubt my mother loved me. She just didn't know how to show it. Who would have been her role model? She and her brothers had been sent to live in Catholic school from an early age. Sound familiar? Send the kids away. She didn't have a positive role model, just like I didn't have a positive role model. I could relate.

Plus, it is my firm belief the apology my mother said Jim gave to her wasn't just for her. It was for everything he had put *all* of us through. Everything he had put *me* through! I had to start back at the beginning and remember she'd lost touch with reality. Her fierce sense of denial had taken over years before. I don't think she has the choice anymore to see things as they truly are. Perhaps Jim was working a Twelve-Step program of his own to make amends to those he had harmed.

Observation vs. Participation

So that was step one of my forgiveness. Acknowledging the truth about our relationship allowed me to become an observer instead of a participant. I began to see myself as casually watching the actual visit, allowing myself to love my mom for who she was, with all her shortcomings, and not expect any sort of outcome. By doing this, I had peace during my visits with her. Peace going in, and peace going out. I observed without engaging. It is not always about me. She honestly had no idea why I was so angry. It was time to let her off the hook. The interesting thing was that I became less "excited" about our visits. When I was in my own process of denial, imagining that I could have the kind of glorious visit with the mother I'd always wished I could have, the anticipation was greater. Now my expectation of the visits had become more realistic, and I became much calmer.

This was a very difficult time. I had to come to terms with the fact that I would never have the mother-daughter relationship I longed for that I saw other people having. I no longer resented people for having the kind of healthy relationships I had lacked in my youth. That resentment was beginning to turn to joy for them. I was learning to let go of the idea that I would have that someday for myself. I learned to grieve the death of an imaginary relationship even though the person had not died. I was carrying around the idea that this would change, and I needed to release her from my expectations. I began to understand it wasn't that she was unwilling. Somewhere along the way, she became unable.

I could let my resentment and rage go. Big exhale. I was demanding a change from her, sometimes very loudly, that she could not give me. It hurts me now to think of how much anger I hurled at her. It's hard to say at what point her unwillingness became inability. Her level of denial was fierce and held her captive. I was now able to look at her with the same compassion as I would a sick friend. She, too, had a highly critical, detached mother, a husband who beat her, unfulfilling relationships, and no real friends. I now see she was incredibly lonely. I saw I had become her, just as she had become her mother. I can see her in my mind walking down the street in her smock with Glenda from next door to the candy company where she worked for minimum wage. She never complained about it. I can see now that she tried. She gave me everything she had. She just couldn't give what I needed.

I was angry at my mother. Voicing those words to myself and the acceptance they brought me was the beginning of my freedom. I had to learn to be mad at who I was mad at and let everyone else off the hook. For decades, I had rage hidden just below the surface. I'm guessing saying it was hidden may also be an exaggeration. I was pissed off and carrying a heavy load from it. It cost me relationships. I'd unleash fury over what most people would view as a minor infraction.

I allowed rage to consume me as I ruminated on situations, past and present, and thought about how I should have handled them. I wanted to hurt people and wield power over them to let them know, in no uncertain terms, that I not only existed but was a force with which to be reckoned. What I didn't understand then was I wanted to hurt my mother the way she'd hurt me. Why didn't she love me? Wanting to hurt her and love her at the same time created nothing but turmoil, a war within. While seeking motherly advice she was incapable of giving, I also wanted to let her know she could no longer tell me what to do.

There were three major turning points in healing that set us both free:

1. The first is outlined above from Joyce K. when she suggested I try to view my mother as a sick friend. Joyce pointed out to me that my mom had not become who she was intentionally and probably didn't like herself very much. My heaping condemnation on her wasn't helping her as a person. I was constantly reminding her that she had failed.

2. The second came when I heard a speaker at an AA meeting suggest that when we have a relationship with established behavior patterns, and we have an expectation that it is going to change, we are likely the ones who are driven crazy by it. Getting frustrated because someone is doing something that they have always done should make us look in the mirror for the source of that frustration, our own unrealistic expectations.

3. The third was learning to grieve the death of the ideal mother-daughter relationship I so deeply craved. I could grieve the death of the idea I had in my heart and mind, even though the person had not died. I mourned the loss of a maternal parent who would hold me, teach me about

life, and encourage me. That parental influence wasn't my experience, and all the anger in the world couldn't change that. When I accepted that fact, I set both myself and my mother free, though I could not discuss any of this with her. To her, I had just become a nicer person to be around. Her defense mechanisms were locked solid. I had no right to continue to condemn her. Let he who is without sin cast the first stone.

My Truth, Their Truth, The Truth

I had spent years and a great deal of energy making sure my mother knew the truth about how I perceived her failure as a mother. But that was how Teresa understood it. Now, God, in His great mercy, allowed me to see *the* truth. I had been a cruel child with a smart mouth, my only weapon in a crazy world. I ridiculed my mother publicly and embarrassed her in front of her boyfriends, all under the guise of humor. Following each with "just kidding." (Beware of yourself and others if the sentence ends with "just kidding." You're not kidding, and this is a very passive/aggressive way to harm people.)

My mother had accepted every one of my collect phone calls at all hours of the night. She trudged to Western Union countless times in the middle of the night in response to my urgent needs, which were almost certainly always drug related. I either needed more drugs, or we had spent the money meant for bills on drugs. With my blinders off, I could see how devastating it must have been for her to drive over four hours to bail me out of jail, only to watch the elevator door open and see me running in the other direction. I can't imagine the pain she felt on her drive home, four hours ticking away in hopelessness, having signed over the title to her house that she'd inherited from her mother, just to try to save my life. Again. What exactly did I want her to do to pay off her emotional debt to me in full? When would enough be enough?

As I climbed ever so slowly out of that murky mud of long-term rage, I could see the price I had paid as well—angry undercurrents in all my relationships, and the many conflicts and confrontations I had with others. I could see the sad expression on her face as she endured my endless jabs just to spend time with me. She had enough internal moral conflicts of her own without the added burden of my criticism.

With my newfound, clearer vision, I also saw her age. I was still battling a woman who was twenty years younger than she was now, at war with the person she used to be. As I emerged with this self-realization, I met a more mature woman who looked sad, tired, and worn. I had missed the years in between.

I am grateful it wasn't too late to have a friendship with her today. We don't speak of failures anymore, hers or mine. We enjoy each other's company. Forgiving myself for all those wasted years has been a bit more of a challenge than releasing my rage.

The Bible is clear:

> *"Honor your father and mother, so that you may live long in the land the Lord Your God is giving you."*
>
> —Exodus 20:12 (ISV)

However, the Bible does not insist that I stay so long in that environment that my parents' old way of thinking starts to make sense to me again—and to this day, it still can. My developmental years were spent in a victim and poverty mindset. Just because I've experienced freedom and enlightenment as I've pursued Jesus and healing doesn't mean I don't have the propensity for victimizing myself when I'm over-exposed to contrary thinking. We are creatures of habit and comfort and will naturally migrate to what we know. We will fall for the same lies over-and-over again unless we actively take steps to pursue righteousness.

"...whatever is true, whatever is noble, whatever is right, whatever is pure, whatever is lovely, whatever is admirable–if anything is excellent or praiseworthy–think about such things."

—Philippians 4:8 (NIV)

Once I learned how to be mad at who I was mad at, the rest of my relationships benefited as well. I was less angry and, therefore, less likely to zero in on perceived flaws or offenses. I became less suspicious of people and just allowed them to be themselves. I no longer silently demanded that everyone agree with me before deciding if they were friend or foe. I could value others for their unique Creator-designed qualities. I could breathe.

I just phoned my mother. At age eighty, she planted a garden this year. We had a lovely conversation about her garden, her beloved dogs, and my transition into retirement. I understand now that time equals love. I lost out on two decades of a peaceful relationship with my mother. I told her I would visit her this summer.

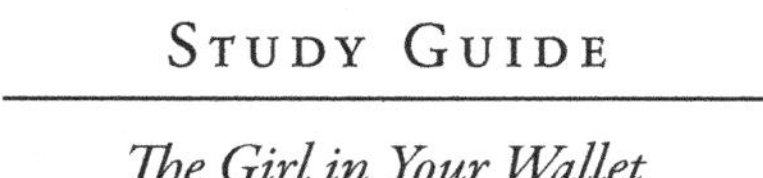

Study Guide

The Girl in Your Wallet

Chapter 20: Mining the Ruins

Forgiveness is vital in the healing journey. I list the following three thoughts that enabled me to move toward forgiveness.

a. God wanted me to. He loved them too.

b. I wanted to.... It was heavy, and I was tired.

c. I understood I could no longer hold other people to a standard I couldn't achieve.

Which one of these is the most difficult for you?

Healing from sexual abuse took time and willingness, but I also sought healing environments where I felt safe, albeit uncomfortable. Describe the balance between feeling safe and uncomfortable (experiencing vulnerability).

Joyce K. would gently remind me of the HOW principle when my temper flared, which was often. Honesty, open-mindedness, and willingness. How would you rate your openness to using HOW in your life?

Are you still holding out for an apology? If so, how long have you been waiting? What relief do you expect it to bring? Is this a realistic expectation?

When thinking of my relationship with my mother, I asked myself a hard question, "Who was truly crazy?" What had I been doing for years that was driving me nuts? How can you relate? Who is the object in your life?

____

____

____

In your own words, describe the difference between observation and participation. Where can you apply this in your life?

____

____

____

Below are the changes in thinking that moved me from participation to observation with my mother. (You may find it helpful to review these each time you spend time with people who can easily provoke you.)

a. Acknowledge the truth/reality of your relationship.

b. Do not expect any sort of outcome during a visit.

c. Observe without engaging.

d. If applicable, grieve the death of the imaginary relationship, the one you keep wishing for.

e. Consider whether they are unable, not unwilling, to say the words you long to hear.

Learning to be mad at who I was mad at allowed me to be a better wife, daughter, friend, employer, and leader. Does a memory still have the power to influence your daily interactions with others? What are the circumstances and beliefs that hold this power?

____

____

____

Are you willing to begin praying to be set free in this area?

____

____

____

CHAPTER 21

Forgiving Myself

"The most profound thing we can offer our children is our own healing."

—Ann Lamott

I HAD HEARD many messages on forgiveness through the years and believed that God had forgiven me for most things. However, I did many things that still brought shame every time I reflected on them; at least three events I had taken part in seemed unforgivable.

The first and most glaring was giving up my son. What mother does that? But it goes deeper than that. I carried the guilt of it around like a lead weight—an internal trophy for the worst mother on the planet. I had talked in-depth to my therapist and Leslie about my feelings of guilt. They both offered very sound perspectives that brought me some level of peace and understanding. My therapist told the Biblical story written in 1 Kings 3:16-28 (NIV).

King Solomon was settling a dispute between two prostitutes who were mothers of infants residing in the same home. One of the babies died, and the deceitful mother switched the live baby with her dead child. The other mother knew the dead child was not hers. The two women took their problem to King Solomon for resolution. He ordered that the remaining child be cut in half and a piece be given to each mother, knowing that the true mother would rather give her child away than see it harmed.

It's an ancient story, and I had trouble relating to it. After reading many Bible translations of it, I could begin to see my desire for what was best for my child played a role in my decision to release custody of him. This story helped show me that my decision to give my child a stable and safe life had been an act of love. In my case, I chose to save him from the childhood I had endured. But I still didn't feel that noble about it.

Leslie asked me if I realized that I, as a rational, well-adjusted adult, was judging my twenty-two-year-old self, an emotionally damaged, intoxicated young woman, for being irrational. She said, "It took you years to get to this place, and you are holding your younger self to a standard she couldn't possibly have achieved."

What she said helped, but freedom from this finally came from a phone conversation with my then twenty-six-year-old son. I was again apologizing for being such a crappy parent, and he had heard enough. "Just stop it. You did the best thing for me," he insisted. "When are you going to realize that? I see young girls all the time carrying their babies into parties. They weren't ready to be mothers, but they are trying to have it both ways. You didn't do that. You gave me a shot. Isn't it time you forgive yourself? Every time you call, I get excited when I see it is you, and then the dread sets in. I know I am going to have to listen to your long list of regrets again. I want to talk about what's going on with you now. I am over it. The only forgiveness you need is for yourself. Do whatever you need to do to remember that. Maybe get a tattoo—I don't know."

So that is what I did; I got a tattoo on my right wrist. It is the Chinese symbol for "forgiveness." It truly worked, as I see it a thousand times a day. I confessed and repented to the Lord my deepest, darkest secrets, and I was set free in this area. The irony is that God already knows. The truth will set us free, but we need to own the truth about ourselves. I am so very grateful I became ready. I am thankful I had some honest people available to hold up the mirror and show me what I couldn't see for myself. I also find it ironic that the one person on earth I thought could never forgive me showed me how to forgive myself. My son had moved on and challenged me to join him.

I found it much easier to forgive others than to forgive myself. I could forgive the girl in my wallet because she was too young to have known anything, but I couldn't forgive my teenage and twenty-something self. It was ridiculous really; I still didn't have any role models or training, but I had nothing but disdain for her. It is the gift of hindsight, sobriety, and experience that has allowed me to begin to remove the bricks from this wall.

God has allowed me to be healed suddenly from some things, but this has not been one of them. It took years to uncover this awareness and then a lot of time to heal. Awareness, acceptance, action. No wrecking ball came through this wall. It took pulling out one brick at a time to release this level of self-hatred.

To forgive myself completely, I had to begin with the same principle I had applied to my mother. I had to view my younger self as a sick friend. Yes, I had been very sick. I had been in the throes of an all-consuming addiction. Over time, working with my therapist, I was able to see my younger self needed some compassion too. Would I treat a woman in a Twelve-Step group like I was berating myself? Never. I would welcome her with open arms. As a group, we would offer her phone numbers to get connected. So, why couldn't I show myself the same compassion I would give a stranger? Slowly I moved out of hatred into understanding and then into a place of compassion. After a time, it became gratitude. Yes, gratitude.

I have a photo of myself in front of the apartment where I was smoking that crack pipe. I've hung it on my bathroom wall. Every time I glance at it, I say thank you. It was difficult at first. I didn't mean it, but I did it. Then I was able to get more specific. "Thank you for being strong enough to survive. Thank you for the memories and experiences that now enable me to relate to other women who are hurting. Thank you for teaching me what I needed to know. Thank you for enduring. You can rest now. We are safe."

I hope you'll notice the emphasis on time in the preceding passages. God, and my own willingness, determined how long I spent in each season, and there were surely setbacks. Having experienced it myself, I'm patient with the ladies in class at the prison. Recovery is not a linear process. Up and down. Forward, backward, forward again. It takes time. I would have brief periods of growth and understanding, only to backslide, picking up the long-entrenched disdain for my younger self without even knowing it. I'd have to start again. "Thank you for being strong enough to survive...." I heard a pastor say the two main reasons people are separated from God are 1) They are mad at Him for not resolving some situation, or 2) They are so ashamed they don't think they can be forgiven. I would agree. But, hopefully, I have demonstrated that you can be set free.

STUDY GUIDE

The Girl in Your Wallet

Chapter 21: Forgiving Myself

Our inner critic can be relentless and brutal. I could not forgive myself for failing my son. Who was finally able to help me see the effect of carrying around that guilt?

____

____

____

Are you wearing yourself out explaining your position or apologizing to someone who has already made their mind up? How long has this been going on? How can you begin to apply some of these principles?

Moving from self-hatred to understanding and then into compassion took a great deal of time. Where are you in this process?

I took a tangible step to change my thinking by thanking my younger self—by being grateful, even when I didn't feel it. Take some time and inventory your thoughts about yourself. Using my examples, can you replace that thought with an adult truth?

Self-Hatred Thinking	**Forgiven Gracious Thoughts**
EX: I was/am so stupid when I hurt people I love.	I made a decision with the information I had. Until now, I did not know another way.

CHAPTER 22

Damaging Relationships

"You get hit the hardest when trying to run or hide from a problem. Like the defense on a football field, putting all focus on evading only one defender is asking to be blindsided."

—Criss Jami, *Killosophy*

WHEN I SPEAK to prison classes, I use my examples of what happened after I was released from jail and treatment and I had begun to change my life. I feel it would be irresponsible to convey that a desire to change is enough. We all encounter difficulties. We always will.

Three significant relationships impacted me. One I saw coming, one I should have seen coming, and one I did not see coming at all.

The one I saw coming was with Curtis, my son's father. We shared a child, so I knew I would encounter him again. Several years after becoming sober, I drove over to Christopher's grandmother's house for Thanksgiving dinner. I knew I would see the family, and I was scared to death, but I was willing to do it anyway.

I arrived and was sitting at the table, making small talk, when Curtis came in. I was shaking so badly that I had to forcibly push my hands on the table to stop the trembling. He came in and was joking about some of the good old days we'd had, and, yes, we'd had some. I did my best not to engage, and at some point, his mother asked me if I would go to the store to pick something up that she needed. I told her sure. When I looked out at my car, I saw Curtis had blocked me in. He knew every other person attending and what cars they drove, so his parking position was purposeful. I was trapped. His answer was, "I will just give you a ride." There was no way I was getting in the car with him, and then it escalated until he said, "What do you think I'm going to do? You're ridiculous. Why are you making such a big deal out of this?" As he became more and more obstinate, I could hear my sponsor in my head telling me, "Do not engage; pray; stay calm." I was still holding my hands on the table because I was trembling. Finally, his brother spoke up and said, "I'll go to the store. Don't worry about it."

The second relationship I should have seen coming was my relationship with Mark. All the signs were there that marrying him was a bad idea, but as I've said, inmates make great boyfriends. I believed everything he told me, even though his behavior did not line up with what he said. When he was released from prison, it was an entirely different story.

The third damaging relationship I didn't see coming was with a close family member. I was blindsided. After all the years of hearing I needed to get my sh-t together, I thought he would be supportive. I had yet to recognize that whenever I was with my family, I automatically assumed my role: third child/mere female/powerless, and I would snap into that position. In turn, they took their well-established roles as well. I had no value or worth. I had endured so many lectures about how terrible a person I was that I thought he would be happy. Now his approach was to invite me to a birthday party at a bar and ask why I couldn't at least have one beer. When I told him I wasn't going to go, he let me know how boring I had become. That hurt, for sure. I wanted him to like me and support me, but I wanted sobriety more. Then came the reminders: I wasn't better than anyone else, I shouldn't forget where I came from, and

I had turned out worst of all (this was true, and I had to own that). Then he listed all the things I needed to do with my life.

The irony was he was not leading a life I admired or respected, or that he seemed even to be enjoying, yet he felt the need for control over mine. He went on to tell me I would likely fail like I always did. Yeah, that hurt too, but I didn't have to own it.

Freedom and peace come when you can learn to hear potentially hurtful information (especially from someone you love), yet use your own filter to determine whether the information is truthful or useful. This information was not. It was descriptive of my past, and I was choosing not to own that in my current life. I was changing—I knew it, and God knew it. Since I'd become a Christian and was learning little by little how to submit control to God, it was easier for me to be lonely for the sake of not going back to the life that I tried so hard to leave. I could be lonely for the sake of freedom.

Brick by Brick

I had been a Christian for many years, and I had seen God's promises fulfilled in my life, but there were still blockages. Sometimes I would hear a message in church or on the radio or in a book that made me notice a separation between the full glory the Bible said I could have, what I saw other people experiencing, and my own experience. I still had many false beliefs that caused this, and I would have to challenge these issues individually.

One big issue seemed to come up over-and-over again: the abortion issue. The more exposure I had to churches, both in person and on my television, the more messages I heard about abortion. The truth is everything I understood about the Word of God said I was guilty of having done this once. I did it at least three times, and I didn't feel bad about it. Not even a little. What in the world was wrong with me? I was defensive about these decisions.

As God typically is with me, He was persistent. The issue came up again and again, and I finally faced it. Confrontation in this instance meant crying out loud for revelation. How was I supposed to get through this to the other side when I had no remorse? Wasn't repentance dependent on remorse? Did I misunderstand how this whole thing was supposed to work?

Totally spent from finally releasing with words what had been pent up in my spirit, my mind opened. My heart became willing, and I could at least admit that I wondered what type of people those children would have grown up to become. Since I looked at the world with a different set of eyes than many other believers who may not have experienced this personally, I felt very alone and isolated. Different. Separate.

I sat at church home groups where opinions were shared that made it all sound so simple. Say no to sex, no problem. That was not my experience. My experience was more like a hostage situation. I continued to put on my game face and go through the motions. I just kept quiet. I stopped going to groups in some cases.

I could see the pro-choice supporters out there and wondered if some, like me, had chosen abortion or were they just in support of the idea? Had they experienced those quiet moments when it was just them and their Creator and wondered what could have been? Would they have had a boy or a girl? What would be their hopes and dreams? Could they have changed the world? Could they have changed me?

I began to have glimpses of this kind of thinking and heartfelt reflection, but I couldn't stay there for long. It was overwhelming and fleeting. I could only handle a little at a time, and God was merciful to dole it out in increments. A wall remained that I could not identify, but I believed God was answering my prayer, and I asked him for continued revelation.

The adoption process would have invited authorities into our lives, and was to be avoided at all costs. That was a principle instilled in me from at a very young age. It would require meetings, questionnaires, doctor appointments, and all manner of accountability, exposing our illegal and dysfunctional lifestyle.

Slowly, over time, it occurred to me that I couldn't imagine these aborted fetuses as happy children because I didn't believe they would have had a shot at happiness. I was so incredibly miserable and was being physically abused and so emotionally destroyed that I felt that would be their fate as well. The deciding factor in giving up custody of my son was that parental behaviors are passed down to the next generation. I could see the future. One day the switch flipped, and I understood. I had no remorse for these children I had aborted because, in my mind, I was saving them from the same fate to which I had been sentenced.

This clarity came in a rush. What a crazy, mixed-up world where I believed that killing someone was saving them. But that was the truth. That was my truth. I could not save my own child who had been born. He was witnessing the emotional abuse and drug abuse I had experienced as a child and felt he was destined to a life similar to my own. I wanted so much more for him. In total honesty, I was an unfit mother. How would I have been anything other than critical, emotionally absent, and short-tempered? I had not had one positive role model from which to draw. I was loaded every chance I had, under the influence of some mind or mood-altering drug or alcohol—anything to kill the pain and allow me to tolerate myself. I was isolated from the world, and in my much-distorted thinking, I was freeing these unborn children from my fate.

With this newfound clarity, I fell to my knees and praised the living God who loved me despite these choices. I had felt hopeless and had aborted innocent children. I could now feel the regret for the acts themselves and compassion for my younger self for not knowing how much God loved me, then and now. I could wholeheartedly repent and ask forgiveness for the lies I believed and my actions. My heart softened and opened just a little bit more. I have a great deal of compassion and empathy for those who face the same decisions.

I hear the pro-choice/pro-life debate. We all do. While I don't advocate the pro-choice decision, I understand there are a million reasons why that woman ends up at a clinic. One day I may show up outside an abortion clinic with a chair and a sign that reads, "I just want to give you a hug. Been there."

Because of my experiences, it can be challenging for me to interact with the church community. I need to remember people speak from their own position and not take everything personally. I do not have a sign above my head listing my sins. Neither do you. Note: I mentioned the above references to time for a reason. How much time does it take to learn and heal from this level of sin and forgiveness? As much time as it takes. I had been a Christian for more than fifteen years before I addressed this issue.

If you think your issues are just too big for God, you have a distorted view of the Father. Pursue that biblically:

> *"...he rewards those who earnestly seek him."*
>
> —Hebrews 11:6 (NIV)

Teachable Moments

Focusing

I was in a yoga class, and we were moving into a pose that required a tremendous amount of balance. One arm forward, the opposite leg back, standing on the other. I remember looking in the mirror, watching my body shake all over the place, trying to hold that position. The teacher told us to focus on an immovable object and that the body would adjust. Sure enough, I focused on the seam where the mirrors met in front of me, and I became very still, balanced, and stable. It was an eye-opening experience to see my body snap into position. And yet, the same is true of our walk with the Lord. If we stay focused on the *only* immovable object, we can be still, focused, and balanced. I wish I could tell you I remember to do this all the time, but that's not the case. My experiences sometimes must get quite painful before I get back on track.

Listening

I was running errands on Saturday and had multiple stops. As I was rushing about my ultra-efficient day, I headed into the Christian store to buy a new Bible because my dog ate the cover of mine (yes, really). I asked the young man where the New Living Translation Bibles were. He was very kind, walked me to the aisle, and asked me what I was looking for specifically. I remember thinking, "I don't have time for all these pleasantries. I just need a Bible so I can get on with my day. I have stuff to do."

At that very moment, I was overcome with the clear thought that I was selecting the Word of God, the very Word that changed my life, the book containing sacred Scripture written for my benefit, for my teaching past, present, and future. Was God truly just part of my to-do list? No, of course not. I felt my heartbeat slow as I recognized His presence in my experience. I silently asked His forgiveness and thanked Him for joining me.

The young man I was speaking with was very knowledgeable, and I began listening to what he was telling me about all the reference materials. He showed me how to read the notes in the margin and other things I had never noticed before. I took my time and selected the book through which God speaks to me, my Bible.

As I turned to go, still humbled from this experience, I noticed a couple of rows down, there were personal Bible studies. Among them were the small pamphlet-sized studies usually based on a biblical topic of some sort. At that moment, the Holy Spirit provided me with a memory of myself eighteen years earlier, taking a great deal of time selecting one of these types of studies. At the time, I was a brand-new Christian, and $6.00 was all I had. I was careful and selective. He showed me a glimpse of the road we had traveled together. In His compassionate style, He showed me I had abided in Him, and in return, He had abided in me. He is faithful. If you seek Him, you will find Him. And what's more? He is waiting for you!

"And without faith it is impossible to please God
because anyone who comes to him must believe that he exists
and that he rewards those who earnestly seek him."
—Hebrews 11:6 (NIV)

Trusting

We can learn life lessons anywhere if we're willing. It also helps to have a sense of humor. Scott and I have two little rescue dogs. Sadly, Munch'k doesn't ride in the car well. As soon as we back out of the driveway, she begins to shake, which progresses quickly to heavy panting and frantic jumping from seat to seat. Then, incessant whining sets in. By the time I get to the vet's office, a mere two miles away, I'm sitting in a car filled with hot dog breath, irritated, having tried in vain to reason with her. She's a little happier when we get out of the car, but as soon as we hit the smells of the vet's office, she shifts gears into the next wild level. While I sit with her, I try my best to keep her from hunching up and dropping a doodle in the middle of the lobby. I speak softly, "Munch'k, I am not going to let anything bad happen to you. I have always taken care of you, right? You don't have to lose your ever-lovin' mind, Sweet Pea." This does not change her behavior one bit. She's still freaking out, jumping up and down, crying like crazy, starting to froth at the mouth.

Like Munch'k, I still have bouts of anxiety and have accepted that may just be the way it is. Maybe it's my own personal version of a thorn in the flesh. It strikes me that God has said the same things to me that I say to Munch'k over goodness-knows-what while I shake, whine, jump around, and freak out. It still amuses me that, despite my high maintenance, He still has a sense of humor. I imagine Him sitting in a cloud, smiling benevolently, holding me as I hyperventilate with my smelly breath, saying, "I am not going to let anything happen to you. I have always taken care of you, right? You don't have to lose your ever-lovin' mind, Sweet Pea!"

Whatever you magnify gets bigger. Magnify your problems they get bigger. Magnify your God and He gets bigger. Period.

Study Guide

The Girl in Your Wallet

Chapter 22: Damaging Relationships

As you move forward to make a positive change in your life, who has or who do you think will make it harder on you and who will be on your growth team? Who has surprised you?

____

____

____

Sometimes, our growth makes others uncomfortable, and they may say hurtful things. How have you experienced this? Can you evaluate the information as truthful or useful before you allow it to hurt or sway you?

Is being lonely and unpopular a price you are willing to pay for the sake of your freedom? Why or why not?

God slowly and gently brings up issues as we are ready. The work continues. In what areas can you relate to my thinking about my abortions? How has this encouraged you?

God speaks into the everyday moments of our lives. Of the three teachable moments, which one ministered to you the most? What did you learn?

CHAPTER 23

Seeking Help

"Kindness has converted more sinners than zeal, eloquence, or learning."
—Frederick Faber

I OFTEN HEAR Christians discount Alcoholics Anonymous for its loose stance on a Higher Power and, as a Christ-follower, I understand that argument. I hear some things in meeting rooms that are contrary to my belief system. I also hear them at the grocery store, at the auto shop, and on Facebook, so I don't get stuck there. *I strongly believe anyone seeking help for addiction should be encouraged to begin where they are, and the group they join should be the one they will attend.* God will direct the steps of the sincere seeker.

I had burned every bridge to every relationship I had, so I didn't have anyone criticizing my choice of recovery support program. That may have been a gift. My entire life I believed I wasn't good enough, so I can't imagine being hindered by my team of "supporters" weighing in and saying that my choices to try to get cleaned up weren't good enough either. I went where I felt I fit in and *where I felt accepted.* Time and time again, I have sat in these rooms and heard the devastation of addiction. When the speaker is finished at Alcoholics Anonymous, we say, "Welcome. Thank you for sharing. We are glad you're here." *We will go where we are accepted.*

I attended an orientation at a church-based recovery program recently. Among other things, I learned their protocol was that if you are offended by someone's sharing, you can raise your hand for them to stop. While I understand the thinking behind this, in the hardened condition I was in when I first arrived, if someone had raised their hand because they were offended by what I was talking about, I would not have returned. This would have only reinforced the idea that I had to clean up first to be good enough for church. We will leave where we don't feel accepted.

Hopefully, I have effectively outlined my misconception about the church and its members, the "good" people. In contrast to everything I had been taught and then confirmed about myself being bad, I might never have gotten clean and sober if the Christian-based program had been my only option. We must be careful not to encourage someone to change and then discourage or micro-manage them by shooting down the method they choose, especially if that method has a substantial success rate.

If you think you heard me say "anything goes," then you have missed the message here. I don't endorse any treatment that forces the participant to vomit or become very ill while serving them alcohol. In my experience, behaviors are changed by changing beliefs, not by causing physical pain. I am pretty sure we understand that when we stop taking the med, the vomiting will stop. We are alcoholics, not idiots. But I refer to the paragraph above. If that is where you begin, and you are sincere, I believe God will meet you there. I wish you nothing but the best. I hope we all make it.

God took my first, sincere steps and guided me in the way He decided. I went to treatment for all the wrong reasons, yet it was the first step to changing my life. It was my AA sponsor who led me into a relationship with Christ. It was Mark's AA sponsor who invited us to church and Bible study.

I saw a meme on Facebook recently that said, "Treatment: where you spend $15,000 to find out meetings are free." I heard this in meetings for years, mostly from people who didn't have an opportunity to go to treatment. They walked to school, barefoot in the snow, uphill both ways too. Remember the slogan, "Take what you want and leave the rest." Shake that stuff off. You do what's right for you. Check in with your Creator; He has a plan. Our role is just to take the next indicated step.

"Do not despise these small beginnings,
for the Lord rejoices to see the work begin."
—Zechariah 4:10 (NLT)

Relating to One Another

Sometimes, it is simply a matter of understanding you and another have had different experiences so do not measure yourself against each other. As a mentor, you may have been mortified at a meeting for forgetting someone's name. To your mentee, embarrassment was being strip-searched: lift your breasts, shake out your hair, spread your butt cheeks, and squat and cough. It doesn't make anyone right or wrong. You are just not relating to one another. We need to let each other off the hook. It is not a competition.

I Had to Stop Judging the Church

As I mentioned, I was taught that the church was where the "good" people socialized and learned of God. I had also been taught that I was not good. This confusing message created "us and them" before I even drove onto the property. I was conflicted between a hunger to learn of God and the people who inhabited the building He resided in. I had an attitude of "You can't understand what I have been through."

Although a lot of times that was true, there was also an underlying problem with looking for others with the same level of wounding I had endured. Yes, we understood each other, and there was a comfort in that. It also meant, in many cases, I was surrounding myself with people who weren't growing. I desired joy and peace in my life, but I viewed those who were not miserable as out of touch with reality. It was a vicious cycle that left me isolated and either feeling sorry for myself (nobody understands me) or hanging out with the "same ole, same ole" crowd that was going to spend a bunch more time commiserating about...how nobody understands them.

I've tended to seek out the pain in people and disqualified them when they didn't express it. I can tell you one thing for sure, seek out people who have what you want! If I wanted peace and joy, and I did, I needed to stop leading a meet and greet with how much suffering I had endured. Let me save you some time. If we are alive on planet earth, we have suffered pain.

The Church Had to Stop Judging Me

How do we, as the public, and especially the church, respond when a woman tells us she has been recently released from prison? Are we repulsed and think, "Not on my pew!" From what I hear, it might be more common than you think.

In 2016, an estimated 40 percent of all women released from Washington prisons were likely to re-offend within two or three years following their release. Forty percent of all women returning to prison is sad, but we can infer 60 percent of the women released do not return to prison and, to some degree, reintegrate themselves back into society. For most, it is not an easy transition. With their prison record, these women face resistance in many ways—finding work, finding a place to live, social stigma, etc. I have experienced this to a much lesser degree, but these women persevere. Today, there seem to be more organizations that look past the prison record stigma and welcome these women back into society. Sadly, the local church may not always be one of them. Some local churches seem to applaud or support the concept of helping former inmates but adopt a "Not-In-My Back-Yard (NIMBY)" attitude when asked to provide direct help or to support these women publicly in their congregations. Hey, it can be scary to think your family may be sitting next to a criminal. The truth is, they may be there already, but without the freedom to be honest.

In theory, we all have the capacity to be a criminal. How much better for everyone if we could just be honest with each other, recognizing that we're all sinners. Just a thought.

I believe most of the churches I have attended would welcome the newly released to the best of their ability. The problem with the church is that it is full of flawed people. I know this for certain because they let me in! The people serving at my church come from various backgrounds, but you can't tell their history by looking at them on Sunday morning any more than you can tell someone else's story anywhere else. We need to remember that the problem with the church is that it is full of people. Flawed, every single one. Imperfect, forgiven and trying.

Being Judged

I clearly didn't know how to behave. Why in the world are they passing a bucket around? I was trying so hard to mimic everyone else's behavior and drum up some manners that I fumbled all over. I didn't know how to tell people a little about myself without blurting out a bunch of random facts they hadn't asked for. I did this to a poor unsuspecting soul early in my sobriety. He went silent on me, and I filled my mind with all the horrible things I imagined he was thinking. I look back now and think he was likely just speechless. Shock will do that to you. There was nothing subtle about me.

I dropped an F-bomb in the church parking lot. Yep, that was me; sorry. It had been a part of my speech my entire life, and the endeavor to change that was like learning a different language. I didn't want to be offensive; I wanted to change, but first, I had to learn the definition of offensive. To do as the Romans do, we must first learn what the Romans do. I had to remember I didn't need to show my resume or tell my life story to attend church. Neither do you. Leading a workshop on how to go to church at the women's institution has been one of my most rewarding experiences.

Study Guide

The Girl in Your Wallet

Chapter 23: Seeking Help

A recovery program will fit if it has a success rate and you will attend it. We will go where we are accepted. We will leave where we don't feel accepted. If you are trying to help an addict, are you micro-managing the method/program/frequency/behavior they use to get clean and sober? How can these insights enable you to become a better coach and friend to those struggling?

Initially, it was tough for me to go to church. It is also hard for the church to know how best to support newly released inmates or addicts. What do you think needs to happen to make this easier for both?

____

____

____

Have you ever held the church as a whole responsible for some of its members' actions? Is this a fair analysis?

____

____

____

CHAPTER 24

Healing the Past

"The idea that you have to be protected from any kind of uncomfortable emotion is what I absolutely do not subscribe to."

—John Cleese

Fearing Rejection

FIRST, is the possibility of rejection real or perceived? I know what it feels like to be rejected by those who should have accepted me. I know what it feels like to be told not to forget where I come from, that I'm no better than anyone else, and to know my place. I know what it feels like to so desperately want to be one of the cool kids, only to be shut out. It was a fact that I was rejected by those who should have protected me.

What about perceived rejection? What about when I imagine a specific process and outcome and don't get it? Based on your body language, your tone of voice, and your inability to play your role correctly (one I made up), I can falsely believe you have rejected me. In return, I reject you right back. This imaginary scenario plays out in my head before the experience ever happens if it happens. By the way, this is exhausting. No wonder I am so tired.

Fact: I don't know what you're thinking. I know that people

process information in their specific God-given way. We are extroverts, introverts, intuitive, fact-based analyzers, and more. We process data based on personal experiences and what we have come to believe about them. We are all unique in numerous ways. Somehow, I had the preconceived notion that others should and would respond to situations and information as I did. When they didn't, I took it personally.

God can also use rejection to create boundaries for me. What appears to be the rejection of people may very well be God guiding my path to something different. It is His world, and He is in control of it.

Recently, in my efforts to interact with my Christian sisters, I facilitated a video-driven Bible study at my home. It started with about fourteen women every Tuesday evening. In the beginning, we had a couple of ladies who were very vocal and shared often. Others were more reserved. Some were silent. I kept the conversation going. I wanted to get to know these ladies a little better.

An interesting thing happened to our group dynamic. As our attendance fell, some of our original, very interactive ladies quieted down, and some of our quieter ladies spoke up. I had a choice to make in how I viewed this information. My first inclination was to run out and gather those we had lost. Were you offended? How can I get you to come back? Ultimately, the inner question I would never say out loud was, "Why don't you like me?"

I don't spend long in this cycle anymore, but it still runs through my head. The truth is some may not like me. It is statistically impossible that everyone will like me. This fact makes me a little sad, but nonetheless, it remains true. It's okay. I am not everyone's cup of tea. I am acceptable, and I am enough. I get to be authentically who I am, and they get to be authentically who they are. It's not all about me.

As the study went on, attendance dropped even more. I released myself from the responsibility of overthinking their reasons for not coming. When I saw a couple of the women at church, one disclosed a life crisis had pulled her away. The other admitted the subject matter hit a little too close to something she wasn't ready to deal with. It turned out it wasn't all about me.

As I called on our early contributors to share a couple of times, I heard, "I am thinking through this material and what she just said." Another said, "I really feel like God has asked me to learn how to become a better listener." And "I'm sorry; I didn't get much sleep last night." Again, it's not all about me.

Our ladies who engaged a couple of weeks into the study turned out to be our introverts. They needed to evaluate the room and see how the interaction played out before engaging. They also needed a silent moment to begin, and we extroverts don't do well with silent spaces (you know who you are!). As some of us were quieting down, we created room for them to share. There was also a level of trust they were considering. Was this a safe place to share? In one example, a mother and daughter came. Mom was an extrovert and started strong. Her daughter remained silent. Mom also did not stay for more than a couple of weeks. After she left, her daughter engaged. I have no idea what the dynamic was there, and I don't need to know because it's not all about me.

All of this is to illustrate that I could have taken offense at many of these issues and felt rejected or slighted. I need to remember I may be the center of *my* universe, but I am not the center of *the* universe. However, getting it from my head to my heart is a process.

Learning Your Triggers

My suggestion to you is that if you are angry, spend some time finding out why. James 1:5 (NIV) says, "If any of you lacks wisdom, you should ask God, who gives generously to all without finding fault, and it will be given to you."

It is not fair to ask those who love us to walk on eggshells because we are not willing to deal with the truth about ourselves. If you are one who says, "This is how I have always been," just turn that over to the One who has always been. Your issues are not secret to Him and likely not to those around you, no matter how well you think you are holding it together. He will not leave you with a revelation without the compassion or guidance to deal with it. I honestly thought digging into these painful issues would either kill me or leave me exposed and vulnerable for all to see. Neither happened.

I have struggled with people who have similar personality characteristics to those who had power over me in my youth. It has happened several times, and I will outline one example for you here. Slipping into this felt much like the PTSD episode I described earlier.

John was the new general manager of a restaurant chain that bought our bread. When he took over the position, he requested a meeting with me. Since this was a normal operation for my job, I showed up calm and confident. However, I was unprepared for what happened. When I arrived at the restaurant, a hostess seated me in a booth. From behind me, John charged into the dining room, and in a booming voice, he brashly called out, "We need to get some things straight from the start!" I was startled, to say the least. When he came into view, he stood over me, still blasting me with his words. As I rose to shake his hand, he told me to remain seated. He stayed standing. I sat, silenced.

The baffling part is that I have no problem with confrontation. If anything, it comes easily to me. So, why in the world did I allow this man to intimidate me into agreeing and apologizing for everything he perceived as inadequacies in our company? He and I were just meeting for the first time. Why did I allow him that kind of power? I had fired customers before for poor working relationships when it wasn't mutually beneficial to the company, or they weren't respectful of us. Why not now?

I wish I could tell you I snapped out of it and pulled myself out of my submissive stance with this guy. But I did not. I spent two years tiptoeing around him. Plus, not only did I tiptoe around him, but I spent a lot of time coaching our delivery drivers how to coddle him and training employees handling our order desk, who cringed every time he phoned, how to suck up to him. So, what was the deal? What happened? Why this guy?

To say my staff was confused is a major understatement. They knew I demanded respect for myself and all our employees, so their confusion turned to frustration when I singled out this one customer, nowhere near our largest, and cowered. The fact was I had met in John a representation of a close male family member. Loud, arrogant, and obnoxious. The similarity had caught me off guard, and all my ingrained childhood behaviors had kicked in. I assumed my well-established position in the family: third child/mere female/powerless. My role in the family was to keep the peace, be agreeable, give them whatever power they wanted, and be invisible. I didn't begin to understand what had happened to me personally until much later. My business relationship with John ended later for different reasons. I did learn important lessons from that relationship (and others like it) at a great price of pain and time.

Ask yourself: Is there someone who knocks you off-balance? Are you drawn to the same type of person over-and-over again? Do you feel restless, irritable, and discontented around them? These are warning signs, and you may want to look at your choices. Or, better yet, ask a good friend or therapist to share their perspective. Before you ask, make sure your friendship can withstand some truth-telling. You need "truth-tellers" in your inner circle.

My best advice is to stay on your journey of self-discovery, not as the lofty spiritual quest it is sometimes hyped-up to be in the media, but as a way of learning your strengths and weaknesses and being compassionate with yourself about them. By examining past behaviors, relationships, and triggers, you can troubleshoot sooner where you might get tripped up.

I find now that I recognize those patterns much sooner, nearly always. When I do stumble, it's usually because I placed power in an individual's hands rather than keeping Jesus at the helm. Note: I did not say the other person took power. No one can take power from me. Whatever I magnify gets bigger, and when my view is horizontal, I know I am headed for trouble. When I put my hope in God, however, I live in His strength and power.

Facing Your Bad Influences

During the holidays, like so many other people, I miss my family. Or, better put, I miss the "idea" of family. An honest trip down memory lane reveals a family that included me, but that withheld love and manipulated each other to get attention or their way. The attitude, "I will speak to you or grace you with my presence if you meet my expectations," always took precedence. When the expectations are ever-changing and never clearly defined, pleasing others becomes futile and exhausting. Their requirements remain unspoken and change with the wind. True communication becomes impossible because it requires people holding power to release it, and they aren't willing to let it go.

I'm not going to sugarcoat this struggle. When you love your bad influences, it can be very tough. Some of us don't have to look outside our bloodlines for bad examples. Even though we know it, we will often go to our death defending them. I have learned to love my family from a distance, both in miles and frequency of contact. I made an agreement with myself a long time ago that if I do not have enough money for a hotel room when I visit, I do not have enough money to go. I require a place of retreat while doing my best to honor my family. Nobody said it was going to be easy. Yes, I miss my family and pray for them regularly. A little loneliness is a small price to pay for some serenity.

Changing Your Belief Systems

Whether you are an inmate, former inmate, drug addict, or someone who wants, for any reason, to change your life, first recognize that you matter. If your sense of self-importance is akin to an apology for using air to breathe, like it was for me, I challenge you to think of a time when you were backed into a corner and came out fighting. The pressure built, and maybe you surrendered for a while, but then suddenly it was "game-on." You knew you were going to lose, but you came out swinging anyway. If that's all you have, start there. That is your God-given survival system. God made you, and you matter, regardless of what you or anyone else thinks about your difficult beginnings or current situation.

You are hand-selected by God to be here, right now. You are not an accident to Him, and in the core of your being, if you know that is true, and you are willing to fight for it, that can be your first connection to value.

Behaviors originate in our thinking:

> *"For as he thinketh in his heart, so is he."*
>
> —Proverbs 23:7 (KJV)

Our actions always stem from a belief we hold. My mother taught me I could never survive without a man. I believed her. Deep down, I also believed Curtis when he told me no man would ever want me unless he were a drunk in a bar. Ironically, these were the only men I noticed checking me out because I carried that belief. This same belief prompted me to go to bars again and again. As an alcoholic, I could get booze anywhere and for less money. I was lonely and believed the only men who would want me would be in a bar, so I frequented bars in an attempt to fill that void.

I have poured out my life story to you to show you I had to unlearn as many things as I learned. You can do this too. The messages I received as a child were delivered by very damaged, hurting people. They were not the truth, but I accepted them and repeated those messages long after the people were gone. I hope you won't wait as long. What is true is...you were planned by God, you are loved and lovable, accepted and acceptable—yesterday, today, and tomorrow. Be kind to yourself and keep moving.

Who Do You Say You Are?

When I identify myself with a certain group of people, be it social, psychological, or economic, my natural inclination is to behave the way I perceive those people behave. If I continue to call myself a high school dropout, addict, or poor, I align my behavior accordingly. It's a self-fulfilling prophecy. What I expect to happen will happen. I will make sure of it. If I am stating facts in a historical narrative, then these statements are accurate. If I use them to describe who I am, they are defeating and stifling my ability to grow.

Here is where I will contradict myself: Whenever I attend an AA meeting, I always introduce myself as an alcoholic. My position is this: I am only one drink away from active addiction. I have heard many people in AA come back to the program after they have relapsed and have lost everything again in a short time. The descriptions I hear are that they immediately went back to the same level of devastation that drove them to AA in the first place. I don't need to learn every lesson on my own. I am all ears to learn from those who have gone before me. So, when I introduce myself as an alcoholic, I acknowledge I have nothing on that woman sitting next to me who is shaking with the hangover of her life. There, but for the grace of God, go I. The person in that room with the most sobriety is whoever got up first this morning and, therefore, has the most time being sober that day. Sobriety and clean time are always one day at a time.

I had a dear friend ask me if I thought I could not drink like a "normal" person after all this time. "You don't think you could just enjoy a glass of wine?" I answered, "Maybe, but there is still an addict in there. Should I risk it?" Nope, not going there. I have been given too much peace and freedom to play with the blessing. I must be careful never to glamorize the past and focus on any perceived good points or imagine my clean and sober life lacks something. It is a lie. I hope I recoil, like reaching for a hot poker, and should the temptation arise, I pray that will always be my response. There is nothing God has asked me to leave behind that hasn't been for my own good. The letting go may have been difficult, but I don't miss it. Getting sober was hard, and as they say, "I know I have another drunk in me. I don't know if I have another sober." If you ever hear me wavering from this position, I need you to call me on it immediately. I need to hit another meeting.

Study Guide

The Girl in Your Wallet

Chapter 24: Healing the Past

What truth do I hold onto that prevents the rejection cycle from replaying in my mind?

I may be the center of ____________ universe,
but I am not the center of ____________ universe.

Digging into painful issues won't kill you, but you do need a support system person and, preferably, a therapist/counselor. Sharing with Joyce K. allowed me to speak from the heart and my current reality, not draw on her observations from my past behavior through her own perceptions or emotions. There was a great benefit to Joyce K. being a stranger. When have you tried to share intimate feelings with someone you know to be met with "what you always do" or even a joke about past failures?

____

____

____

As you read of my encounter with John at the restaurant meeting, what emotions were brought up for you? Give an example of how you relate to being blindsided in this way?

____

____

____

"I assumed my well-established position in the family: third child/mere female/powerless."

When you are triggered, is there a familiar role you revert to from a previous time in your life? (Answering this may take some time; giving it some serious thought can help uncover a pattern.)

____

____

____

Do you have people who tell you the truth with love and grace in your inner circle? If you do, list two here.

I have created a protective structure of limited contact and miles between myself and my bad influences (family), What boundaries have you found helpful? Is there more work to do in this area? Explain.

The truth is God knows you, loves you, and accepts you just where you are. Our thoughts determine our behavior. What statements of fact will you begin using in place of your negative self-talk? List three.

1. ___

2. ___

3. ___

What words do you frequently use to describe yourself inwardly?

In what ways are they manifesting in your current reality? How are they ensuring a "self-fulfilling prophecy?"

CHAPTER 25

Passing It On

"The sacrifice I was being asked to make was significant only in my own head."

—Richard Sterns, *Unfinished*

MORE PROGRAMS ARE available for the releasing inmate or indigent person reentering society in my experience and observation than there are later on. I see many programs posted at prisons that I hope the ladies are taking advantage of, such as addiction recovery, counseling, job search preparation, and more.

I asked our group what other classes were available and made a list on the whiteboard. Many were religious programming and parenting classes, but others began to stand out to me as we went through the exercise. I asked how many courses they had participated in. Sentencing required some classes, so those were completed, but I was surprised by the lack of interest in formal education.

As I pondered this information, the dry erase pen still in my hand, I asked, "Why aren't you attending?" The answers weren't clear, so I clarified my question. "You are required to be here for a set period of time per the terms of your sentence, and many people are coming into this facility to help you. Some, like me, have been successful in their careers and have come back to give you a hand up, to give you a better shot at staying out of here. Why wouldn't you take advantage of that? My question is are you doing time, or are you using time?"

Personally, I took every class available to me that my schedule would allow, and I did it afraid and filled with self-doubt. I knew I needed every advantage I could get because my resume had very little on it, and I was anxious about explaining large gaps of time. I attended those classes along with a committee of voices in my head telling me things like, "You'll make a fool out of myself," or "You're not smart enough." I still struggle in this area, but I no longer feel the negative voices are reserved for those of us who have had to overcome some extreme obstacles. I am convinced everyone faces these types of insecurities.

Finding Your Place

I had known for some time that God was directing me to work with other women, and I knew it would take me to corrections facilities. I visited the county jail with my church ministry only once. The communication with the women there felt more like a desperate plea to us (and God) to get them out of their immediate crisis so they could get on with their lives. I desire to help change lives, not situations. The pain of incarceration was the very thing I needed to be motivated to change. For now, my calling is mostly through the written word. When God has a new mission or modification, I trust he will let me know.

When someone says, "But you're only one person, what difference can you make?" First, I am not the only one by any stretch. Second, even if I were, they still need hope. I'd better get busy.

I felt no apprehension as I entered the Washington Corrections Center for Women. Nervous energy, yes. Fear, no. I had previously spent many, many hours in these types of visiting rooms. This time was different. This time had a purpose. We had a set curriculum and the opportunity to share life experiences, much like sharing with you on these pages.

"But I have prayed for you that your own faith may not fail. When you have come back, you must strengthen your brothers."
—Luke 22:32 (ISV)

We are told to go back and strengthen our brothers. In this case, my sisters.

Passing It On

I asked my class to write down everything they hate about being in prison. There was a very visual and vocal response. As you might expect, there are many things. After the long lists were complete, I asked them to turn their paper over and make a list of what they liked about being in prison. They balked at the idea. While it may sound like a ridiculous exercise, I primed the pump and said, "It is my firm belief that jail saved my life. That would be on my list. I was likely to be dead either by the people I was hanging with or by my own negligence." Then, I asked them to reconsider the question by asking themselves the following questions:

1. While you are here, are you able to avoid that dangerous person?
2. Are you relieved of making difficult decisions?
3. Have you made friends here?
4. Are you relieved of the expectations of others?

I allowed some pondering time, and it took a while, but eventually, pens hit paper, and lists were made, albeit much shorter than the first. I then said, "I believe these are the items that are likely to get you in trouble when you get out of here. When things get hard, we tend to minimize what we didn't like about our previous situation and magnify the small number of good things that happened, no matter how much we hated them at the time. True? Or am I the only one?"

Hebrews 11:15 (ESV) says, "If they had been thinking of that land from which they had gone out, they would have had opportunity to return."

I then shared, "At one point, I glamorized being back in jail, so no one could call, expect anything from me, and I didn't have to make any decisions. Have you, like me, ever dwelled on all the sweet qualities of that man until you 'accidentally' bumped into him again? Somehow you were able to forget or minimize all the heartbreak and landed right back in a situation you had been begging God to get you out of? Yep, me too. Let's wise up this time. Those lists are what to watch out for."

Loneliness can only be rivaled by addiction as the biggest motivation for my poor decisions.

I added, "I want to encourage you to think about what you want, not what you left. Speak about God's promises rather than reflecting with fondness on what you were begging to be delivered from."

Finally, I reminded them, "If we have accepted Christ as our Savior, we are not the same person we used to be. We have no business going where we used to go, even in our minds. We must surround ourselves with God's Word and His people to help us see what we cannot see on our own. Get yourself some people who aren't afraid to tell you when you might be headed for trouble, and then listen to them."

While I didn't think to elaborate on it during the class, if given the opportunity again, I would talk about how God saw fit to provide me with the gift of desperation. My memory and recall of the pain, suffering, emptiness, and being cold, damp, dirty, and hopeless are so vivid that I have never been able to attach any pleasant feeling to it. I had a complete understanding that any "good" things I remembered were only slightly better than the gut-wrenching, painful normalcy of what I'd known. It did not make them good. I was no longer in denial. My motivation was to never, ever experience the level of devastation and pain I was leaving behind. I was not chasing a goal. I was running into an unknown future by way of exiting my past. The work continues.

Yet, I still needed to work some things out with God and a good therapist. I would hear teachings on Philippians 3:13 about "*forgetting what lies behind and pressing on to what lies ahead*" and would internalize that to mean the memories should disappear. They did not. I wondered what was wrong with me. Through time and the experience of walking with God, I now interpret the Apostle Paul's words a little differently. It is not for me to have my memory wiped clean. It is for me not to give the past any energy or power. The past doesn't get to influence today's decisions except to warn me not to repeat them. It doesn't get to own me. By focusing on what lies ahead, I do not wallow day after day in what is done and has long been forgiven. Forgetting in this context means I don't open the door for revisiting.

Lamentations 3:19-20 (NIV) says, "I remember my affliction and my wandering, the bitterness and the gall. I well remember them, and my soul is downcast within me."

That life, those negative experiences, are still available to me should I decide to backslide in my spiritual health. Lies we've internalized and incorporated into our unconscious damage us further if we waste time regretting wasted time. Living in regret serves no good purpose. Sometimes my past can still taunt me, but I recognize it sooner and shake it off. Progress is the goal, not perfection.

Today, I can reflect on my memories without reliving their pain and remorse. AA has taught me, "We do not regret the past, nor wish to shut the door on it." Healing comes if we work through these things. I thought the experience would kill me. It has not. It has set me free.

But It's Not Fair!

One of the biggest hang-ups for me throughout my early years was asking, "Why?" Why did these bad things happen to me? Why did or didn't people do what was fair? Why did God allow suffering? It wasn't until I understood the principle of free will that I could begin to come out from under it. God gives all of us free will, and there will always be some fallout since we are flawed and sinful creatures. It's possible that someone misused theirs, and we were harmed in the process. Fair? Not really, especially when you are a child. You couldn't possibly have deserved it. Here is the rub and what I could share with my class: It wasn't fair! It's okay to grieve that injustice. What you don't get to do is stay attached to that sentiment indefinitely and live in self-pity. This is where we see people give up on their lives and remain stuck.

Have you been around someone who is still grumbling about a person they haven't been married to for twenty years? They dropped anchor there. Freedom came when I understood I had continued the cycle and harmed others with my actions. It was evident in what I went through with my son. When we consider who may have been injured by our own choices, we can begin to let go of the grudges we have been harboring for others. I didn't have to look far to see numerous people I had negatively impacted.

Risking Heartbreak

I was incredibly saddened in my spirit when I watched a long-time student in my finance class build money into her budget for marijuana. She had been a delight and had much Bible knowledge. She had been in drug treatment centers and had confessed she was an addict. In my earthly view, she was headed for real trouble. As I drove away from the facility, I reviewed the class in my mind, as I always did. I cried out, "Lord, I thought she was past this. We have seen so much growth! Why is she still in denial?" In my spirit, I could feel the message. "Your role is not to heal anyone or to even define their healing. Your role is to show them love and share your testimony of our journey together. Stay out of the outcome."

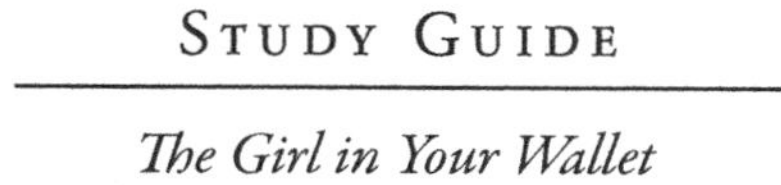

Chapter 25: Passing It On

What classes or experiences intrigue you that you continue to dismiss? What is at the root of not stepping out and learning something new?

I asked the class two questions: 1) What do you hate about being in prison? and 2) What do you like about being in prison? What do you think the purpose was of having the inmates write these lists?

(This exercise was derived from a pastor's message on marriage counseling. He asked both parties to write the items they were frustrated about with their spouse on a piece of paper. After the long, angry lists were made, he asked them to turn their paper over and list what they wished was wrong with their spouse. He was met with confusion and blank stares. This is where the magic lies. Only Jesus was perfect. People will always have shortcomings.)

In what areas can you apply this tool? Relationships? Criticism of your pastors or teachers? What shortcomings would be acceptable?

I share a misinterpretation I held of Philippians 3:13, believing I should have my memories wiped clean, which did not happen. *"It is for me to not give the past any energy or power."* Can you think of a memory that, when considered, knocks the wind out of your sails? Perhaps one glance back at your younger self in that scenario, and all confidence is gone? Write what comes to mind here.

____

____

____

I believe it is necessary to recognize and grieve injustices to be free of them. We don't get to stay attached to that sentiment indefinitely, live in self-pity, and experience freedom. It won't work. Rate your willingness to open up and begin healing—circle one.

a. I am *not* going there.

b. I want to reread my answers first.

c. I am oscillating between "yes" and "no way"!

d. I am willing to see a therapist at least once.

e. Let's do this! People hurt me, and I hurt others, but it doesn't get to own me anymore!

CHAPTER 26

The Empowering Question

"If you do not know how to ask the right question, you discover nothing."
—W. Edwards Deming

IN MY EARLY days working for Bob at the bakery, I asked numerous questions, and doing so offered me a glimpse into the bigger picture. From the outside, it might look like the biggest favor Bob did for me was selling me the bakery. But from my vantage point, most important was helping me become someone who could handle such an experience. He invited me into the big picture.

I am reminded of a sermon I heard about the young shepherd David, who had been anointed (or declared) to be future King of Israel, then went back to tending sheep. For years. Later, he would find himself in the palace, but not yet on the throne. He resided there as a servant for his skill in playing the lyre (a harp-like instrument) to soothe King Saul. For years. The point is this: David was wise and experienced in the fields protecting and caring for his flock. He had an amazing destiny that he was yet unprepared to step into. David did not know how a palace ran, its customs and inner workings. He would indeed sit on the throne one day and his son after him, but he needed the character and knowledge to handle such an experience.

And that took time.

A little at a time, Bob shared some of the goals he had for the bakery and asked me what I thought it would take to get from where we were to where he wanted to be. He asked how his high-level decisions might trickle down and impact the production floor. Did we have enough ovens and racks available, or would we need to split up the order to meet the deadline? Would space allow for that many people to be working at the same time?

Many years later, as the owner of the bakery, I hired a very experienced and highly organized department manager. As a group of five managers, we held meetings every Wednesday morning. We were experiencing success and having a pretty good time doing it, despite facing challenges and inadequacies, and we enjoyed working together. As the discussions broke up, this specific manager would remain seated and inform us that the meeting had not yet concluded. He would then ask a clarifying question.

"What is my role?"

We had high-energy visionary meetings with discussions of new product lines, target customers, or increasing productivity for many years. We left talks feeling great and patting each other on the back, sharing our enthusiasm. All in attendance would return to their work areas, and later, one-by-one, each of these managers would pop by my office to ask for an additional piece of information. We had left without being given the specific parameters and timelines of each person's role: the who, what, why, when, where, and how many, and next step. Until I hired this new manager, I couldn't see the breakdown in communication.

Those pop-in visits broke concentration for the tasks we were working on, essentially delaying the result, and causing distraction.

A quick answer was often just enough to buy some more time. They would be back again for more clarification. Also, not everyone had heard the clarifying answer and was now working on dated information. Around and around, we went.

As we matured as a team, we began to ask the clarifying questions in the initial meeting and repeat back to the group what each person's role was, as we understood it. Often, one person's task would need completion before handing it off to the next person, so we needed to establish an order of events. Because one manager stubbornly sat in the chair and waited until he had all the information, we became better. I became better. This clarifying question of my "role" has proved useful time and time again in business and life. Its benefits are seemingly endless.

I am pleased to have learned this tool, but it sure could have served me earlier in life. If only I had spent more time preparing to know my role with the probation officer during our weekly check-in. I was too busy spinning around what to wear and practicing answers to questions I imagined he might ask to understand I had questions, too. I needed to know some things. I needed to understand my role.

What about the job interview? We can get so nervous about getting the job that we leave without knowing what is expected. How many times do I get caught up in the excitement of a moment and need to make a follow-up phone call or text the next day because I left without all the necessary information? When I show up for my first day of work, who is my contact? Where will I find them? Is someone not responding to your message? Perhaps they asked you to call them, and you are sending endless emails instead.

I have yet to master this process, but I have made progress. I am often guilty of overexplaining and somehow believe because I have used plenty of words and a fair amount of time, I have efficiently outlined what I want, but until I close that gap for the listener or recipient, the directive remains incomplete.

In food manufacturing, one of the least favorite things for many of us to experience is an FDA (Food and Drug Administration) unannounced Food Safety Audit. As a consumer, I am grateful to know this government agency is dropping in to see how our food supply is protected. As a business owner, the "unannounced" part is frustrating. Whatever you had on the calendar is now null and void, often for several days. As soon as FDA employees introduce themselves, my office manager starts making a list of my cancellations to discuss rescheduling or whether someone else can cover for me. On one memorable visit, two inspectors attended: one veteran and one in training. Ugh, this was going to take even longer.

Much like the newly hired manager I described above, this newcomer to the FDA inspection team taught me something that has proved to be very useful. Because she was slower and very intentional, I had a chance to witness her process.

To her left, she placed the official requirements for a baking facility inspection. To her right, she had a bound notebook. In the back of the notebook, she had written a list of bullet points. She did not write anything in those last pages of the book, and it was used repeatedly at each facility. Line by line, she read the question/requirement on her left and flipped to the checklist in the back to be sure she captured the information in its entirety. In front of the same notebook, she made her notes for our specific location.

Using this process, she documented the entire exchange so she could be fully confident in her work. I assume she might limit the follow-up questions she experiences when submitting her audit for internal review.

What I viewed as a disruption to my week turned into a beneficial learning experience. I adapted this process to a notebook I carried with me. Many of my sales meetings were in restaurant kitchens with plenty of pots steaming, knives chopping, and personnel shouting information from front to back of house. As the chef is describing a mouth-watering signature burger bun they want us to create, it is easy to get caught up in the kitchen's tempo. I am simultaneously involved in my creativity and how it will become this plated masterpiece. As a result, I often left without all the information, such as when they needed it? Quantity? Would it be fresh or frozen? Did I need to avoid any ingredients/allergens? etc.

So, while I was frustrated by this time-consuming, unannounced food safety audit disruption, it caused me to slow down and remember I could learn something anywhere. How many times do we miss the lesson when adapting to the world's tempo? By taking the extra time and checking the last pages of my notebook to understand my role, I left my meetings with confidence.

I believe this illustrates another example of how God provides what we need to grow in a spiritual sense. When I read the Bible, my role is that of a student, and while reading my Bible is good, pondering the passage is better. Following up with prayer or a commentary causes me to slow down and keeps me in the scripture/topic longer. Taking a bit more time to consider and ask God how it applies to my life today and in the future makes the experience a lot more meaningful, inserting the message deep into my memory to become potentially life-changing. When I share what I have learned with others, my role becomes leader, author, speaker, and coach.

Study Guide

The Girl in Your Wallet

Chapter 26: The Empowering Question

In what areas can you look back and see you were being prepared to be the person who could handle that great opportunity even though you were unable to see it at the time?

Describe a time you became so excited about a new opportunity that you left the conversation without all the information. How can you incorporate the Empowering Question into everyday life?

How can you adapt the process the FDA inspector used into an upcoming informational exchange? What event, meeting, or appointment on your calendar would benefit from using one of these tools? How?

CHAPTER 27

Life Plan/Target Fixation

"Where there is no vision, there is no hope."

—George Washington Carver

DURING MY TIME in the Pierce County Jail, one woman assumed the role of being in charge of our block. Several times throughout the day, she would make a declaration: "They cannot keep me here forever. What they don't realize is they have given me time to perfect my crime. I'm just in here figuring out where I slacked off and let myself get caught. If they catch me again, I will just have more time to work on it."

I didn't think much about it at the time, but those words would come to mind time and time again over the years. Twenty years later, in a business class, I learned a name for it. Her declaration was a *life plan.* She was casting her vision for an ongoing life of crime and incarceration. I suspect what she spoke into existence and focused on is exactly what she got.

Declaration: a formal or explicit statement or announcement.

This principle would come to mind again later in a motorcycle training class. The exercise was to maneuver the motorcycle at a slow speed through a path lined out by orange cones on both sides. We were instructed not to hit any of the cones but also not to look at them. It seemed ridiculous, and many of us snickered at the idea. How can you avoid hitting something when you're not looking at it? The application was quite different, however.

We quickly learned that whatever we were looking at and were focused on is precisely what we would hit. We had to look at where we *intended or desired* to go to get there. We learned to look at the road ahead, not where we currently are. We learned the term "target fixation."

According to Wikipedia, target fixation is "an attentional phenomenon observed in humans in which an individual becomes so focused on an observed object (be it a target or hazard) that they inadvertently increase their risk of colliding with the object. It is associated with scenarios in which the observer is in control of a high-speed vehicle or other mode of transportation, such as fighter pilots, race-car drivers, and motorcyclists. In such cases, the observer may fixate so intently on the target that they steer in the direction of their gaze, which is often the ultimate cause of a collision."

The Bible talks about the power of the mind and words. We are saved by confessing with our mouths that Jesus is Lord. I believe the words of Philippians 4:8 were written to keep us focused, positive, and optimistic.

> *"Finally, brothers and sisters, whatever is true, whatever is noble, whatever is right, whatever is pure, whatever is lovely, whatever is admirable—if anything is excellent or praiseworthy—think about such things."*

There is a wonderful story in Genesis 13, where Abraham and his nephew Lot part company because their group has grown too large. Abraham, graciously, offers Lot the first choice of the land, saying, "*If you go left. I will go right. If you go right, I will go left*" (Genesis 13:9, NIV).

Lot chose the land that appeared better, so it would be tempting to label Lot as selfish, but the Bible makes no such distinction. I think this is noteworthy. Lot was given an option and chose. He need not be labeled. But before Abraham began to move in the other direction to the land that would become his, the Lord spoke to him. He said, "Lift up now your eyes at all that I will give you" (Genesis 13:15, NIV). I can't see what is ahead if I am looking only at where I am.

I would also like to suggest lifting up our eyes keeps us out of trouble. It warns us about the wrong focus. Thinking about the things we don't want or things we don't want to repeat may very well lead us right back to them. Or, right back to him, *the guy we were begging God to get us away from....*

When the bail bondsman rearrested me in 1992, I had been using meth non-stop for many days and had not slept. I was sobbing all through being rearrested, driven to the jail, booking, and arriving back to the same cell block: another strip search, fingerprint, and photograph. I was tired, spent, and wrung out when I stumbled back in.

The reception I received was hostile and vocal. The ladies who had been there before I was released were still there, and they believed I had been in meetings with the officers to share all the jailhouse gossip with them, then been "replanted" back in the cell to listen for more. The idea still baffles me; I didn't give a crap about these women in the least. Not for their welfare or their harm. They thought an awful lot of themselves, except one.

A familiar face showed up at the door to my cell as I made my bed. It was the same woman who had made the daily announcements about perfecting her crime. The one who had assumed the role of the leader in our block. She stared at the floor and whispered: "What happened out there?" I responded, "I don't know. It happened so fast. They opened the door; I took off, and now I am back here. It's a blur. I don't even know how long I was gone." There was a quiet moment. She nodded at the floor and said, "Yeah...I get you. It happened to me too. Don't worry about these a--holes; I got this."

Assuming the same stance, volume, and tone I had heard every day from my previous stays in the county lockup, she made an announcement. She would not tolerate any more of their crazy theories and told them to leave me alone. Although we continued to share the common space, we never spoke again. We were not friends. We shared a common experience, a moment in time—one addict to another baffled by the compulsion to use drugs and destroy ourselves. I thanked her in the only way I knew how—I quietly walked by and placed a bag of M&Ms on the table in front of her when I received my next commissary.

The Big Book of Alcoholics Anonymous was the first book I studied, the one that led me to the Bible. Purchased in 1992 and given to me by my counselor, I carried it back into the Pierce County Jail with a magnifying glass following completion of in-patient drug treatment. Now, the binding is broken and easily falls to two passages that I grabbed ahold of early and that were life-changing for me. The first made me understand that desire alone wasn't going to relieve me of my addiction: "This is the baffling feature of alcoholism as we know it, this utter inability to leave it alone, no matter how great the necessity or wish" (Chapter 3). My example in jail above, the one shared by my fellow inmate, still serves as a reminder that I am not cured of addiction. My ability to lie to myself remains in-tact and can lead me right back there if left unchecked. Conscious knowledge of my condition and focus on the right things is still required to safeguard myself from relapsing.

The second passage from my *Big Book* that deeply implanted itself in me was the knowledge that I would need to focus on and maintain a relationship with a power greater than myself if I was going to keep that freedom. In this book, I have outlined my initial spiritual experience and the curiosity about God that began as a result. My role is to stay focused and to stay in a teachable mindset.

Study Guide

The Girl in Your Wallet

Chapter 27: Life Plan/Target Fixation

Have you ever found yourself rehearsing a bad decision to make it better next time? What end result were you (or are you) trying to manipulate? Why do you want it so badly?

____

____

____

Even if you do not have a formal life plan, most of us recite something we want or don't want regularly. What result are your recurring thoughts or declarations centered around?

____

____

____

How does your answer above line up with Philippians 4:8? Is your focus on what is positive, or does it carry a heaviness?

Does your life plan seek immediate satisfaction or have long-term implications? Will it benefit your children?

CHAPTER 28

Removing Labels

"The world is not fair. If you persist in presuming it is, you will create a lot of unnecessary misery for yourself."

—Fred Green

IN 2007, TWO years after I had taken over ownership of the bakery, I contacted an attorney about having my criminal record cleared. I was providing forty-plus jobs in the community and was a long-time local homeowner. It was relatively uneventful; I paid the attorney, and it was over. Or so I thought.

In 2008, my criminal record showed up on a background check required by a customer. I explained it had been a drug conviction sixteen years prior and had caused a course correction in my life. He and I had done business together for several years, so he knew me. He was required to discuss the incident, document it, and it was over. No problem.

I couldn't let it go quite that easily. I contacted the attorney again, and he did a search. He found my record had been sealed everywhere in the state, except the county where I had been arrested. That record also showed every original charge, not just the one for which I had been convicted.

My attorney and I again entered a Pierce County Superior courtroom. I watched as the ladies from jail entered wearing their gray jumpsuits, shackled together, for their arraignments. I was unprepared for this trip down memory lane but held it together. My attorney introduced me and my petition. Jobs were on the line, and, in his words, I was an "exemplary citizen" and a "model of rehabilitation."

The prosecuting attorney then rose to her feet and forcefully opposed my petition. Essentially, she told the court once a criminal, always a criminal, and that label should remain. The public had a right to know who I was, and that identification was mine to bear. Thankfully, the judge disagreed and granted my request, mentioning I had paid my debt to society.

The entire exchange took less than two minutes, but I was marred by it. What had just happened? When we reached the hall, I conferred with my attorney. He commented that prosecutors deal with the criminal element all day, every day. They see a lot of the same faces repeatedly. It's a tough job, and they can easily get stuck in a cycle of pessimism. He told me not to take it personally. We had got what we wanted. I understood on an intellectual level, but morally I am still bothered by it.

How much more "rehabilitated" could I have been? I was an accomplished businesswoman who had walked into that courtroom to take care of a legal matter. I was met with a verbal assault on my character by a total stranger—one who had authority.

I think about the women in the courtroom that day. Were they listening? Is it ever really over? Did they wonder why they should even try? If we are trying to make a go at living an honest life, where is the grace? Do we, as the general public, add additional time to someone's sentence by denying job opportunities and more?

My story may seem unique, but I would like to suggest we would hear more success stories if we didn't have to hide this part of our history. I lived a double life for years, carefully dodging questions without being dishonest. I was able to take a position with a small, family-owned company making $5.00 an hour (minimum wage at the time) because their pen-on-paper job application didn't ask if I had been convicted of a felony. I would work my way up to own that same company eleven years later. The owner gave me an opportunity just like everyone else.

Most inmates will be released at some point. We can fear them, or we can mentor them. Of course, it's okay to be cautious and selective. Yes, have some specific structure in place for her to follow. She understands rules and that there are repercussions for breaking them. But without grace and opportunity allowing her to transition from inmate to citizen, there's a greater chance she will add another label to her identity: perhaps homeless, drug addict, or institutionalized.

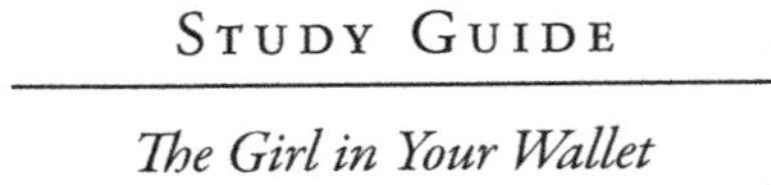

Chapter 28: Removing Labels

What part of my experience in the courtroom surprised you most? Why?

Describe a time when you thought you were meeting expectations and were met with criticism for falling short. What were the stakes? What did you have to lose? What does a releasing inmate have to lose?

CHAPTER 29

Trusting God to Work Out the Details

"When you go through deep waters, I will be with you."
—Isaiah 43:2

IT'S SCARY FOR me to understand I took ownership of the core beliefs I learned in childhood from observing others. Observations through children's eyes and minds are accepted as truth and can be carried an entire lifetime unchecked. What devastation they can cause. I used to be completely opposed to looking back. "What was the point? It is what it is. Stop feeling sorry for yourself. There is no point crying about it now." That was my idea of a pep talk to myself. Now I can't entirely agree with that thinking. We must look back, take that step, and expose it to God's light. Grieve where necessary. Only there can we begin to apply Romans 12:2 (AMP): "Do not be conformed to this world but be transformed by the (constant) renewing of our mind."

I am still a little rough around the edges, very straightforward, and to the point. God is still working on me. I can be abrasive and plow right over the top of people in conversations. So thankfully, God has also taught me how to apologize well and often. I have had a lot of practice. I also recognize the root of some of my bad behavior that I still struggle with today as "landmine issues" because I don't see them coming. I will be strolling along just fine and, suddenly, some random event happens, and I seem to lose my mind. It's an unreasonably destructive reaction. For me, it happens when I feel slighted, overlooked, or ignored. The little girl in me can be triggered, and my inner survivalist emerges in an instant. I am immediately that young, defensive woman, and I become very vocal and angry. I am no longer powerless and invisible, and it happens less, but I have yet to master it.

I have often sat in rooms where the vocabulary exceeds my own. In the past, I would have been intimidated by it. I have now reached the point where I can generalize the meaning based on the subject of discussion or a word's use in a sentence. Or I sometimes ask the speaker to clarify what they mean. When I do the latter, I am always surprised when someone thanks me later because they didn't know what the speaker was saying, but they were too embarrassed to ask.

These are the types of issues you can only deal with when they happen and, through the power of the Holy Spirit, not react to them destructively. It is like exercising a new muscle when you're in that situation. Adrenaline pumps and reactions automatically go into play. If you have the presence of mind to listen to The Still Small Voice, it also speaks.

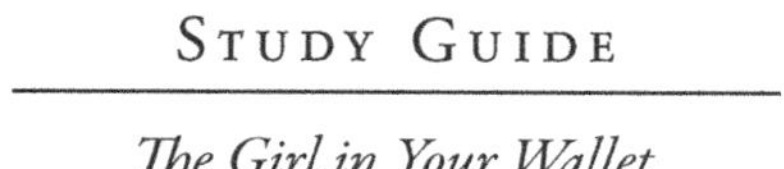

The Girl in Your Wallet

Chapter 29: Trusting God to Work Out the Details

What are your "landmine issues"? Example: feeling ignored, overlooked, or slighted.

How has this book challenged you to consider the power of your self-talk?

Romans 12:2 (A.M.P.) says, "Do not be conformed to this world but be transformed by the (constant) renewing of your mind." This verse suggests this turn around is not a one-and-done action.

List three tangible ways you can "constantly" guard yourself about a negative internal dialogue. (Example: Note on the bathroom mirror or dashboard of your car.)

1. ______________________________

2. ______________________________

3. ______________________________

CHAPTER 30

Mentoring

"One person can make a difference and everyone should try it."
—John F. Kennedy

MENTORS COME INTO our lives when we are ready for them. Mine have been amazing. In the beginning, I simply observed hardworking, forthright people who obeyed the law and paid taxes. Later, after I accepted Jesus as Savior, they were people who walked out their faith by showing generosity and giving their time and resources to helping others.

In my opinion, mentors don't always need to be on top of their game, highly educated, and ready to impart wisdom. Sometimes they just need to be there for you as a consistent presence and guide while you sort things out. They can encourage you to make wise choices, lead you back toward your core values, and help you strengthen your personal and professional relationships. You are the one who will need to take ownership of your own decision-making. A good mentor will encourage personal responsibility.

To mentors, I would add that while we do change behaviors by overcoming our belief systems and that mentor influence is desperately needed, please understand that your immediate advice and well-placed Scripture may not be well received. Change takes time. Be patient.

Helpful Mentoring

I heard a story of a teenage girl who had broken up with her boyfriend and been laid off from her first job. She was devastated. Heartbroken and depressed, she retreated into her room. Her well-meaning mother took on the task of reminding her daily of all the things she had going for her, telling her she was pretty, popular, and smart. This mother and daughter became more and more frustrated with each other. The daughter felt the mom didn't (or wasn't even trying to) understand, and the mom couldn't understand why her daughter didn't just "snap out of it." When the daughter was asked how she was getting along with her father, she said, "Great. He isn't trying to change me."

In her grief, the daughter seemed to have sunk into a dark, damp well with only a small circle of sunlight visible way up at the top. Now and then, Mom would poke her head over the edge and yell, "You're pretty, you're popular, and you're smart! Come out of there!" How was Dad handling it differently? He crawled down into the well and just sat with her. Some days, they were silent. Sometimes, he held her while she cried. He offered her nothing but his love and presence.

The point of this story is mentors don't have to be all-knowing. Sometimes advice is the last thing people need, and a well-intended Scripture does not a clean slate make. Telling someone who is in a great deal of pain that "God will work it all out for good" is just confusing. We need to go through, not around, and it's harder to do it alone. Often, they need to know you care, which can be demonstrated by your time and presence, and not withdrawing from them if they choose not to follow your guidance. I am very thankful Joyce K. did not abandon me as I suffered the repercussions of my poor decisions.

Some advantages result for the alcoholic or drug addict who attends a Twelve-Step group that does not appear readily available in other places. AA places great emphasis on finding a sponsor (or mentor), whether your brand new or you've been attending for twenty years. Achieving and maintaining sobriety is greatly enhanced with another person to connect with, reason things through with, and have a familiar ally in life's struggle.

Those of us in Twelve-Step programs may have an edge on secret-keeping as well. Nearly all Twelve-Step groups end their meetings with the following (or a very similar) statement: "Anonymity is the spiritual foundation of our program. If we are to recover, we must feel free to say what is in our minds and hearts. Therefore, who you see here, what you hear here, when you leave here, let it stay here."

We understand that we are responsible for returning the confidence if we want our personal information kept by others. This remains true whether the relationship dissolves naturally or by conflict. While there is no such thing as perfect adherence to this policy, I applaud the effort to remind the participants.

Many churches I have attended place great emphasis on small groups, and rightly so. It wouldn't hurt to provide those same small groups an outline on Safe People—how to spot one and how to be one. (Again, check out *Safe People: How to Find Relationships That Are Good for You* by Dr. Henry Cloud and Dr. John Townsend.)

So, how do you find a mentor if you're not an addict? I have two suggestions that may be helpful. One is to ask advice from someone who has dealt with a situation similar to whatever you are now encountering. Asking what they may have done wrong is just as valuable as what they did well. If you decide to take their advice, however modified, follow up and let them know how it went. This is a great compliment and may invite more conversation. Perhaps ask them to coffee once in a while and let it evolve from there. It need not be formalized and labeled with a great deal of structure, such as Joyce K. and I shared. Contrarily, a formal label may cause many people to believe they require some formal qualifications or a large time slot to be available.

A second suggestion is an adaption from a Saturday morning AA meeting in Washington I attended for many years. After reading the "Twelve Steps" and "How it Works," there is a call for those available to sponsor. "If you are available to sponsor, please raise your hand." This simple act allows those who admittedly have time and are willing to reveal themselves, which significantly reduces the risk of rejection. You still have to ask. The action step belongs to you.

Perhaps the two ideas could be blended for small groups or Bible studies at church. For years, I've attended many video-driven Bible studies with eight participants at each table. Perhaps, there could be a sign-up sheet or an invitation to have a one-on-one call with a group member every week outside of the formal gathering to get to know one another. Perhaps these "homework partners" could agree to speak to one another at least once before the next meeting to discuss whatever they wish. By the end of eight weeks, each person at the table would have had a private conversation with every other participant.

These are merely suggestions, and maybe you can modify them into something of your own; isolation truly is the enemy. No matter how awkward it may be, we need community.

I strongly suggest you have more than one person you consult and confer with regularly. Since we all experience periods of sadness, backsliding, and rebellion, having only one source of guidance is risky. Depending on how difficult their struggle may be at the time, if we blindly follow the advice of only one person, we might well find ourselves down in the dumps and backsliding too. I hear women often say their sister or aunt is the only friend or support system they need. My question is: Is it fair to put that much pressure on her to live her life and feel responsible for yours too? You may find her pulling away as she lacks encouragement to share with you at that moment since she can't give away what she doesn't have. I think our mentors deserve more grace than that.

I regularly volunteered at a program for women and children

moving out of homelessness. These courageous women are stepping out into the unknown with the hope that life can be different for them. Though their backgrounds vary, there is brokenness and pain at their core. We show up anonymously and transform their cafeteria into a dining room to help them celebrate their graduations to the next level in the program or from out of the program completely. Many have a history of drug addiction, abuse, and possibly criminal records. They are very polite as they try to show us how grateful they are. They are beautiful, courageous souls. No sound is more rewarding than the laughter when they arrive in that room with their families to celebrate.

This evening is a reward for their hard work and having met the requirements of the program. They have earned a shopping trip in a room of donated formal wear and shoes from a well-known department store. Local makeup artists donate their services for the big day. How wonderful to feel beautiful and glamorous for a couple of hours and celebrate with their families. We applaud them this evening.

At one such celebration, a very timid young woman came for dinner, found the room transformed, and was seated by a server. She looked very uncomfortable and asked me what was going on. I let her know we were there to serve them Christmas dinner. Clearly even more confused, she asked, "Why?"

Why? At a very basic level, I want women like her to realize we are there simply because they matter. I don't know her name and may never see her again, but I love her. It's an honor to give away what was so freely given to me when I needed it most. Was it really twenty-nine years ago that I first walked into the treatment center blind, broken in spirit, with homemade tattoos and bad teeth? I see my past in her and have experienced what God can do. Don't give up hope! Glory....

Loving hearts may want to accelerate the process and get these ladies on their feet as soon as possible, but it must happen in their own time—and in God's time. He sets the priority of what needs to happen first and last. Perhaps He is building their character and lessening their burdens to be able to handle the experience. I certainly don't need to burden them with my interpretations of what they should be doing. I just need to love my neighbor.

Those Who Have Blessed Me

I have benefited from observing and spending time with many kind souls. As I said before, there is a difference between role models and mentors. In my early years, I modeled behavior after the only examples I had and ad-libbed the rest. You have seen where that got me.

A mentor is defined in *Merriam-Webster Collegiate Dictionary* as "a trusted counselor or guide." Trust takes time. It is much easier to listen to someone if you have spent some time with them and know they only want what is best for you.

My teachers included Joyce Meyer, Beth Moore, Dr. Henry Cloud, and Dr. John Townsend. I have learned much from Alcoholics Anonymous and my selfless sponsors within the program. The people mentioned below were also significant because after my eyes had been opened by Alcoholics Anonymous and the accompanying spiritual awakening, I observed and chose to regard these individuals as worthy of emulating. Many more people have influenced and helped me, but I selected these for a reason. They did not provide my every need or even give me advice. Most would tell you they didn't even know this is how I felt about them. Yet here they are, written from my fondest memories.

Below is a partial list of the kind souls I have benefited from observing and spending time with throughout my recovery. Keep in mind, what they didn't do was as important as what they did. You can take what you want and leave the rest.

Joyce K. (1992-1995)—My first AA sponsor. It couldn't have been easy for her. I was angry, hostile, and broken. She would be the first person I would be completely honest with and remain in a continuous relationship with. I fully expected her to end things whenever I disclosed more of the ugliness that had been my life up until that point. She never did. She did not abandon me as I continued to make poor decisions, nor did she feel sorry for me when I suffered the repercussions. I wouldn't understand until many years later what she meant when she said our time together was keeping her sober.

What she taught me:

- **Acceptance.** We were very different, yet Joyce K. demonstrated the essence of AA's live-and-let-live level of acceptance. I disclosed my ugliest confessions, and she didn't flinch. She didn't try to fix me. She cried with me.

- **Personal Responsibility.** Joyce K. taught me to focus on my actions and feelings and not blame others. As we went through the entire fourth and fifth steps, she consistently redirected and stopped me from including the roles other people had played in the storyline. I learned I was responsible for my actions, and I needed to own them. Yes, circumstances played a role, but ultimately, I had choices every step of the way.

- **Patience.** I can't imagine what it must have sounded like to hear my plans to marry Mark while he was still in prison. She offered me plenty of suggestions on slowing down and settling into this new life. She suggested I wait a year, which was a common suggestion within the program, which I also disregarded. I went through with my plan, and she remained the same supporting sponsor.

- **Live in the present.** "You're not there yet" was a common phrase I heard as I anticipated and stressed about what might happen in the future. Fear of an unknown future multiplied by anxiety can certainly take away any peace at the moment. (I'm still working on this one.)

- **Suit up and show up.** Wake up and get dressed at the same time every morning whether you have somewhere to go or not. Try it. It will do a lot for your self-esteem and add structure to your day. Act as if you do have somewhere to be, and you'll be ready when the opportunity presents itself. Or when your probation officer stops by.

Mr. and Mrs. Barr (1995-1997)—The first landlords to whom I did not lie. We rented a little 600-square-foot house with a bathroom so small you almost had to stand in the shower stall to close the door behind you. All the floors leaned slightly downhill at the walls, and I wanted it. $400 a month was a lot of money.

They listened to our sincerity and rented the home to us with no references but my mother's. They brought us a Christmas gift basket every year we were in the house, with unsolicited kindness. We asked if we could put a larger window in the living room to hold a swamp cooler we had purchased at a pawnshop during an especially hot summer. They came and did the work themselves at their own expense and then had the carpets professionally cleaned to clean up the mess.

Tom and Dee (1994-1997)—Tom was Mark's AA sponsor when he was released from prison. He and his wife were generous in a way I had never seen before. They gave of themselves. Tom picked Mark up for meetings, invited us to their home for a barbecue, and invited us to their church, which also included an invitation to a Bible study they led there. We accepted that invitation, but I can only remember two things about it: 1) The name of the book was *The Search for Significance*, and 2), I was so nervous I couldn't speak. Tom and Dee were authentic, positive, and kind. When Spokane was engulfed in ice for days during a devastating storm, Tom and Dee drove over to check on us and see if we had power or needed anything. They said they were out looking for "strays" and taking those who needed help home with them. Tom and Dee's invitation to church followed my accepting Christ during my fifth step with Joyce K. The first church service I ever attended was at Calvary Chapel Spokane when I was roughly twenty-nine years old.

Don Jacox (1998-Present)—I wasn't sure we would qualify to buy a house, but I called anyway, and the realtor agreed to be there on Sunday to show it to me. As I walked up the driveway, a gentleman leaned into his car singing, "God is Good." Although he was not speaking to me and may not have even seen me yet, I replied, "Yes, He is." Mr. Don Jacox turned from the car, delighted, and asked me with great enthusiasm, "Do you know Him?"

I had no way of knowing how long my relationship with Don would be. We bought that house and the next with his help. His spiritual guidance and unashamed love for the Lord will always be his legacy for me. It does not matter who is within earshot. He proclaims Christ as his Savior.

He has counseled me in life, business, and spiritual matters, always bringing me back to Scripture. (Primarily Philippians 4:6-9. It seems I still need to be reminded not to be anxious.)

Barbara (2008-Present)—Barbara was AA sponsor #2. When my marriage to Mark was falling apart, I got my butt to an AA meeting. I had never really been one to speak up, but I had a meltdown then and there. I remember ranting and crying hysterically and then, having purged my frustration, I went quiet. Of course, no one commented directly. That's not how things are done. What does happen is a printed schedule gets passed around for those willing to put their phone number in to call for support, but especially to call before picking up a drink.

The gentlewoman next to me whispered, "That's me," as she pointed to her number. I now had an image of a kind face to go with one of those numbers, and I did call. As you recall, Barbara was the quiet voice on the phone talking me through my major PTSD episode. She was also the one who suggested I wait a year after my divorce before I dated. Excellent advice! I needed to find out who I was before I entered another relationship. My previous choices lacked wisdom. That year went fast, but I am thankful for it. She has been the kind, calm voice of reason for years, and I love her dearly.

Start Where You Are

I spent so many years wanting to help others and then talking myself out of taking any action. I reminded myself of all that I was not; all the Scripture I haven't studied, all the time I didn't have. It was suggested to me that I not focus on all the Scriptures I didn't know and share the ones I did. And time? I will quote Richard Stearns, former president of World Vision, regarding leaving his high-paying job for a non-profit ministry:

"The sacrifice I was being asked to make was significant only in my own head."

Change Takes Time

Following a work-related injury in 2001, I spent four hours a day in physical therapy. I developed a friendship with Becca, one of my therapists, and slowly started letting my guard down. One day, as I walked my cart back and forth across the room, learning how to properly lift a tray of bread so I would not injure myself, she and I engaged in open dialogue about my past. I didn't realize one of the other therapy patients was listening to our conversation. The patient stopped pushing her cart, tilted her head, and said, "But you're so shiny!" In other words, I didn't look like the person I was describing. Yes, I am kind of shiny now. My shininess has come from years of self-discovery, trial and error, sleep, and later, through the benefit of disposable income.

When I was released from the treatment center nine years earlier, I had all the signs of hard living: large gaps between my yellowed teeth, a receding gum line, and acne scars from years of meth use. I had poorly dyed blonde hair with dark roots. I had no idea who I was or how to dress. Lasting change takes time. Be gentle with yourself and those with whom you work. God sees the heart. It will likely take some effort, but we should too.

Study Guide

The Girl in Your Wallet

Chapter 30: Mentors

A good mentor will always encourage personal responsibility. Why do you think that is?

___

___

___

When have you needed someone to just sit "in the well" with you?

___

___

___

How did you select who that was? Were they the right choice? Why or why not?

What do you think I meant by "a well-placed scripture does not a clean slate make"?

CHAPTER 31

Serving Others

"...Here am I. Send me."

—Isaiah 6:8 (NIV)

"I will not let what I cannot do keep me from what I can do."

—Coach Joan Wooden

I WAS TRYING to find my place in serving others many years ago and fumbled all along the way. (For the record, embarrassment won't kill you. Goodness, I just wrote all of this for you to read, and I'm still breathing.) I asked where I could help at church. In my experience, when you are a woman asking a church where you can help, generally, they suggest the children's ministry. This was clearly not my gifting, so I learned to refine my question of how I could help. I was presented with more opportunities, such as entering member information into the church database. Trust me when I tell you not to let me do detailed work with a computer. It was very hard to say no when there is a need, but I must honor how God made me. I was frustrated at not finding my place and pulled back time and time again, but God didn't remove His command to be a part of a community of believers because I was uncomfortable. I encourage everyone, wherever you are, to start there. I had to start walking before God directed my steps. All those years, and He never once tipped the couch over to get me moving. What He wanted from me was obedience. I trust Him to work out the details.

Now I am the proud greeter at the northwest door of my church most Sundays. This is my zone! I relish a friendly "Good Morning" and "Welcome." My very favorite privilege is greeting someone visiting us for the first time, introducing myself, sometimes leaving my post, and giving them a guided tour of the campus within their comfort level. Some want to hear everything, others just the minimum. Some just want to know where the coffee or restroom is. I am reasonably intuitive and tend to sense these things most times. When I don't get it right, I don't beat myself up anymore. It takes all of us to change the world. Besides, what if no one had smiled at me when I walked up to those doors the first time?

Attraction Rather Than Promotion

One of my favorite AA slogans is "Attraction Rather Than Promotion." I believe far more people are drawn to us as Christians if we face them eye-to-eye and genuinely show them love first. It is the principle of "show me, don't tell me." If others see us living a peaceful and honorable life, they will be willing to hear more. I was. We have a far better chance of sharing the gospel and even offering correction than if we accuse and argue. It may feel victorious to win an argument about theology or behavior, but it is fleeting if we leave the hurting soul behind. God will decide what needs to be worked out first. It's not up to me. I am called to love my neighbor.

My interpretation looks like this:

- Grow: Learn what the Bible says about God's heart for the brokenhearted, poor, prisoners, and all who mourn (Isaiah 61:1-2).
- Consider the care of others, whether they are thirsty, hungry, without clothing, sick, or in prison (Matthew 25: 35-36, 46). Ponder the needs for the widows and orphans. (James 1:27). Pray for willingness. Open your mind to what the Holy Spirit will reveal to you and for you.
- Participate: Can you give someone a ride to church? Invite another to Bible study? These are the basics. Can you do more? I wonder what would have happened to me if the alcoholics and drug addicts who came before me had stopped going to meetings. Who would have been there to help me?
- Send: Maybe what God asks from you is financial support.
- Can you donate? I have heard before, and have even thought to myself, that giving money is the easy way out since you don't have to deal directly with those in need. I no longer feel that way. God decides how we participate, and this is a vital step. Prison Fellowship provides books for every participant and leaders manuals, all paid for by donation. It takes money and people working together. You can donate at www.prisonfellowship.com.

I heard a woman at an event talking about giving back at every level of our lives, as we are able. She stood on the platform with one arm lifted to the sky and the other straight down at her side. She lifted her gaze upward and opened and closed her hand as if grasping. She said, "Never forget that you got here by others giving you a hand." She looked down as the lower hand grasped. "There is always someone coming up behind you who needs help." The truth is we all can help, and we are supposed to reach out to others. One person's helping may not look like yours; we are all different, and we are all needed.

I encourage you to try different things and see what God will show you. Don't be afraid to say no if it's not right for you. To those of you asking for help, please learn how to accept "no" graciously. This is a very useful skill.

If prison ministry speaks to you, visit a class with no commitment. I brought a friend recently, and as we left, she said, "They are just women." Yes, they are. Maybe you are meant to be behind the scenes in finance or even in sorting donated clothes. If your gift is organization and written communication, there is a place for you.

What if the funds are there and no one shows up? It happens. An anonymous donor gave a large sum of money to start a seminary at a Washington state prison. We have no volunteers to institute it.

God seems to bring people back to what He has delivered them from, doesn't He? (Emphasis on delivered. I had no business doing any of this until He asked me to. I could have risked relapse.) My life is an illustration of redemption and freedom from captivity, and that is the very place He decided I should go.

On one of my early trips to the prison, I recall saying out loud in my car, "Really, God? I didn't ever want to hear those metal doors slam behind me again." I felt His gentle reply in my spirit, "Neither do those women...go."

After I began volunteering with the women in prison, a thought began to weigh on me often. The directive is clear in James 1:27 to "look after orphans and widows." But when do we stop being orphans? I asked my search engine two questions and received two answers.

1. What is the definition of an orphan? "a child deprived by death of one or both parents."

2. What is the biblical definition of an orphan? This question led me to the Greek word Orphanos: "orphaned or without a father or lacking a guide or teacher."

While my research was hardly scientific, it did reveal what was weighing so heavily on me. We have all heard the saying, "When in Rome, do as the Romans do," but what if you don't know what the Romans do? What if you are well over the legal adult age of eighteen, an arbitrary age selected for when we are responsible enough to be adults, and you haven't yet had a quality parental guide or teacher? I would like to suggest some people are still orphans, in the biblical sense.

Throughout my coming of age, I had role models who provided very little quality guidance. They lived in the house and held titles of mother and stepfather and were under the law to provide a certain level of care, but those who would become a guide or teacher came much later. I was "an orphan" well into my thirties. There are so many others out there like me. Can you mentor some of them?

Mentoring Suggestions

As you begin mentoring women who have been released from prison or even women who are just looking for a helping hand, here are things I've found useful. (Note: I'm assuming you'll be mentoring women, but these suggestions work for men too.)

1. Don't loan her money, give up too many details about your life, or give her your house key. Let's be smart here. If she's in financial trouble already, the likelihood she'll be able to repay you is low. Dave Ramsey teaches that if you really want to help, give money with no expectation of

repayment, and you'll maintain the relationship. Shame will cause the recipient to stay away.

2. Learn to say no in a respectful manner without long explanations of why. Then, don't bring it up again. Having to listen to your reasons why the answer is no and hearing it again and again later just prolongs the awkwardness and embarrassment. It is just painful to keep reliving it.

3. Don't be afraid to let her fail. You don't have the power to cure or ruin anyone. Offering solutions to a person who doesn't see a problem can make you both crazy. You may capture their attention for a minute while they consider if your suggestion has any benefits, but after that, it may be best to get out of the way lest you find yourself injured in the fallout with them. Recovery and successful reentry into society are not your responsibility. You cannot own her behavior. Be there for her, but do not try to prevent the pain of her actions. You may be denying her the very thing she needs to grow.

4. Don't treat her like your child. Being a mentor is not a parental relationship, nor does it make you a person in authority. It is to come alongside, crawl down in the well with her, encourage and comfort them. She doesn't need scolding and will not likely respond well to it.

5. Don't treat her like your drunk uncle or wayward family member who can't seem to stay out of trouble. She is an individual, and just because she may have made some bad decisions, much like whoever it was who hurt you, please don't condemn her for how she let you down. She either got off track or never saw the track, to begin with. But here she is now, and if she is within your sphere of

influence, be kind, go slow, and see how things go. Please don't shine the spotlight on her.

6. Don't be afraid to point out any hostility or ego in a loving manner. It is a defense mechanism used to cover fear. My counselor in treatment said to me on more than one occasion, "I can see that you have a valuable opinion to share, but I cannot receive it when you are this upset and raising your voice. I really want to hear it. Can you relax a little bit and try again? What are you trying to say?"

7. Don't talk at her. She'll be better able to receive from those who begin sentences with: Maybe you could...Have you thought about...I wonder if...Wow, that is tough... what do you think you'll do...and sometimes simply, I don't know, but I would like to pray with you about it....

8. Avoid sentences that begin with:

   a. "What you need to do is...." (Likely, she has already stopped listening and is waiting for your lips to stop moving. If they don't soon, she might walk away while you're still talking.)

   b. "There you go again." (See above. She needs someone alongside her, not someone on a soapbox.)

   c. "This is what you always do...." (You are reminding her that she has not changed, is not likely to change, and you don't believe she can change. You have taken away hope.) A good alternative might be, "Do you think this situation is a little like when ______ happened? Is there something you would have done differently if you could do that again?"

d. Please, do not say, "I read this book, and she says you have to...." No, I didn't. We are all different and should be treated as such.

Remember this key principle that I can attest most addicts understand: We do not respect what we can manipulate.

9. Don't allow yourself to be manipulated. I had no respect for those who just gave away the farm with a sad story. Their stock plummeted right before my eyes. You can look back in your history to see if this has been true for you or by you. Have you ever been disappointed in yourself or someone else who folded when hearing a sad story with a ton of holes in it?

10. Don't have unrealistic expectations. Parole is an extension of the prison sentence, and that can often be overlooked. Most times, it is not over when the offender walks out of the barbed wire. There is a whole new set of requirements and expectations that must be met, or she will violate the terms of release, which means rearrested. There is pressure to succeed in a world that has changed and is changing at a whirlwind pace. Life's decisions have been made for her for a long time, and now she is on her own. I have no problem understanding that she begins romancing the memory of how simple life was inside the prison. She hates it there, but she understands it. There is less pressure. Once the memory becomes sweet, she is in danger.

"If they had been thinking about what they had left behind, they would have had an opportunity to return."
—Hebrews 11:15 (ISV)

We all line up our behavior to support what our mind has decided. I have a friend from childhood who was overwhelmed on the outside after two stints in prison. Her parole officer told her to try harder. Clearly, the parole officer was not listening. My friend went to the drug dealer, filled a syringe with heroin, went back, and laid it on the parole officer's desk. She turned around with her hands behind her and waited to be cuffed. While my friend's example may seem extreme, a willful return to prison is not that uncommon. She hated it, but she understood that world.

11. Don't ask her for all her details too soon (although you will likely want to know if she is a registered sex offender). She will tell you when she's ready. When she does open herself up to you, she will likely be ready for a couple of questions. It may be in the first five minutes you meet... to see how you react. It may come later as she learns to trust you. It may not come at all as she tries to become the person she was always meant to be and not be defined by her crime. Each person is different.

12. Introduce her as your friend. I hope that is what you are becoming.

13. Bake some cookies. I learned this from The Seattle Union Gospel Mission's Search and Rescue team. When the van goes out in the evening to serve the homeless and see if anyone wants to come to the mission to sleep, they take baked goods and hot chocolate. Often, it is an icebreaker. Their recipients will share stories about their mother or grandma who baked, and it takes them back to a pleasant memory—what a great place to start.

Reuniting with Family

I suggest you consult a professional about reintegrating with your children. If they were in the care of a family member while you were incarcerated, they understand established routines. I hear time and time again that once the offender has been released, she's expected to take her children and somehow provide all the stability and parenting they need, day one. Is that truly possible? Just because they saw each other every Sunday afternoon for the last three years doesn't mean the child will do well with the dramatic switch.

I regained the relationship with my son, but I sure wish I would have asked for some guidance. In those early days, we had bumpy phone conversations with awkward silences—the kind between strangers. Years prior, when I signed the final custody documents, Christopher was four years old, and I had not seen or spoken to him in almost all of those missing four years.

There is a big difference in the developmental stages of a four- and an eight-year-old child, and I failed to recognize that. In my mind, I was picking up where we left off. Trying to resume my maternal position with a four-year-old who was now eight created a lot of unnecessary tension and struggle. I wish I would have asked for help. It took a while for me to recognize my situation and then accept the current reality.

We had enough love to keep trying. With Joyce K.'s help, I learned to grieve those lost years and make peace with them, to feel the accompanying emotions of great loss. I could not "make up for the lost time." I had to go through it, not around it. I grieved. Then I moved on healthily. I could see the reality of this moment, not the image I had conjured up in my mind of what it should be or what I wished it was.

Further, I failed to realize the love he held for his father. I won't put words in his mouth, but it will suffice to say he was experiencing emptiness where two parents should have been. It wasn't all about me. He had vacancies other kids didn't seem to have.

My advice is also to create an open line of communication with the child's caregiver. My ex-mother-in-law stepped up and took in her grandchild, and for that, I am eternally grateful. She got him enrolled in school and arranged her work schedule to get him to all those t-ball games and doctor appointments, along with all the other things he needed.

In my little world in eastern Washington, I was busy learning how life worked and pursuing some stability in my life. When I made those periodic phone calls to my son, I had very brief conversations with my ex-mother-in-law. I didn't ask what was on her mind. How was she doing? How could I support her? What was her image of the future?

Hearing the daily play-by-play of what I was missing was difficult, and I may have avoided her for that reason. I can see now how this wasn't helping. If I had opened an easy dialogue with her, perhaps I could have avoided the DSHS garnishment and been pro-active in setting up a reasonable repayment plan. There were more instances where I wished I would have utilized a reintegration specialist, but I didn't know these programs existed. If you need help, start here. http://www.parentinginsideout.org/

Exiting Gracefully

I am often asked if I miss working at the bakery. The answer is no. What I do miss is being a part of something. Since I sit here writing this book in hopes of helping others, I guess I am a part of something bigger than myself and, ultimately, listening to what God has asked me to do.

My brain needs to be quiet to hear my thoughts and receive guidance from the Creator. When I can remove myself physically from my usual routine and go into a personal retreat alone, I get my best results. Without a set schedule, a dishwasher to load, or errands to run, I can focus and find clarity. I still have highs and lows, but I can experience both without believing either is permanent. My low points have become less devastating because as I continue to do the work, the bottom gets raised. The goal is to reach that place of peace in any environment and maintain it. I will let you know if I ever achieve that. Lately, I seem to be taking two steps forward and one step back, which is still one step forward, right?

At one such retreat, during group meditation and after a period of relaxation and stillness, our guide asked us to check in with our bodies. Feeling tense, I lay my hands on my belly and asked myself, "What has you so upset?" As we moved on, our guide asked us to check in with our spirit. I asked, "Lord, where am I out of balance? What is causing this distress?"

Much to my surprise and delight, an answer came to me from the little girl whose photo resides in my wallet and whose spirit lives in me. She seemed to demand to be heard again. She said, "You've learned to protect me from harm and the bullies, but you have not yet learned to treat me with kindness and self-care."

"Why, my soul, are you so downcast? Why so disturbed within me?
Put your hope in God, for I will yet praise
him, my Savior and my God."
— Psalm 43:5 (NIV)

After suffering for more than seven years with numerous and devastating mystery illnesses, I have settled into a much quieter life than my former career could have provided, and the life of a writer suits my current reality. God's timing is never an accident. He is so faithful.

It also occurs to me my inner child's unrest might be that, yet again, she has something to say and no words with which to express it? Could it be she is troubled? The girl in my wallet still lacks the gentleness, structure, and patience of a parent. I believe she called me out for not following through on what I said I would do: to take care of us physically with consistency, gentleness, and boundaries. When the little girl inside you exceeds your adult maturity, it kind of sucks, but so be it.

I have a friend who always says, "People will tell you everything you need to know if you just listen." I believe her. My little girl has always told me what she needs. I have just learned how to listen. Life is certainly a journey with plenty of learning opportunities, and it looks like I'm going to get a second chance at this parenting thing after all.

Study Guide

The Girl in Your Wallet

Chapter 31: Serving Others

One person's helping may not look like yours, but many are needed. When deciding how or where to volunteer, one question to ask is, "What makes me come alive, feel useful, and feel fulfilled?"

____

____

____

Being asked to volunteer and saying no without guilt is hard. Asking someone to volunteer and receiving the no is hard when you have a job that needs doing. What truths help us give and receive grace in these conversations?

How often do you make alone time a priority? Do you invite God into your intimate space?

Do you have a place or practice that allows you to be still and gain clarity?

If you struggle to be still, what is the recurring thought that distracts you?

FINAL THOUGHTS

"There is no greater agony than bearing an untold story inside you."
—Maya Angelou, *I Know Why the Caged Bird Sings*

I have had many experiences that convinced me it was God's will I continue writing, but in closing, I will share three of the main ones:

1. I shared aspects of my life with the ladies at the prisons and shelters as appropriate to the lesson. They have thanked me for my honesty and told me they thought they were the only ones who did or thought these things. I tell them i made it out, and they can, too. God is still performing miracles for the willing, but sometimes he asks us to break a sweat. Risk rejection. Look foolish. Do it afraid. I'm right there with you.

   "For you know that God paid a ransom to save you from the empty life, you inherited from your ancestors."
   —1 Peter 1:18 (NLT)

2. My earthly destiny was the same empty life of my family. These behaviors are generational, as is incarceration. God paid the price for my life, and it is not my duty; it is my privilege to give back. I have enjoyed the splendor of his

grace. It is time to share my path for what is useful. It's god's story. I just play a supporting role. Let's change the trajectory of future generations.

3. Fear of rejection and ridicule have plagued me my entire life. When God called me to this task, this fear was a real stumbling block. Readers of my stories often comment about how brave I am. Maybe, in the beginning, I was. What I am now is free. Whenever I share the story of His healing, restoration, and redemption in my life. My load gets a little lighter.

"He comes alongside us when we go through hard times, and before you know it, He brings us alongside someone else who is going through hard times so that we can be there for that person just like God was there for us."
—2 Cor 1:4 (MSG)

Thank you for joining me on this journey. It is my sincere hope that you are encouraged to step up and step out to work on what may be holding you back. All that is required is honesty, open-mindedness, willingness, and community, the HOW principles.

I hope you will apply the HOW principles to your relationship with God and yourself. There is no hole so deep and no heart so hard that He cannot reach it. My peace came with surrender, hard work, obedience, and the willingness to look foolish. The work continues. I encourage you to review your answers to earlier questions to see if you have a different perspective and perhaps, spend some time journaling about how your perspective has changed from reading this book.

Below is the Seventh Step prayer of Alcoholics Anonymous. It was what led me to accept Jesus Christ as Lord and Savior. That was the day my life changed. He is waiting for you too.

"My Creator, I am now willing that you
should have all of me, good and bad.
I pray that you now remove from me
every single defect of character
which stands in the way of my usefulness to you and my fellows.
Grant me strength, as I go out from here, to do your bidding."

—Alcoholics Anonymous, 1939

REFERENCES/SOURCES OF QUOTES

Batterson, Mark. *All In: You Are One Decision Away From a Totally Different Life*. Grand Rapids, MI: Zondervan, 2013.

Harvey, Steve. *Act Like a Lady, Think Like a Man: What Men Really Think About Love, Relationships, Intimacy, and Commitment*. New York, NY: HarperCollins, 2009, 2014.

Richard Stearns. *Unfinished: Filling the Hole in Our Gospel*. Nashville, TN: Thomas Nelson, 2013.

W., Bill. *Alcoholics Anonymous: The Story of How Many Thousands of Men and Women Have Recovered from Alcoholism*. New York, NY: Alcoholics Anonymous World Services, 1976.

ACKNOWLEDGMENTS

This book is the second edition of the one I didn't think anyone would read. I tried to ensure that outcome by blocking my close friends from seeing the notifications on social media and even considered using a pen name. Imagine that, me still trying to hide and manipulate an outcome. Thankfully, I failed, and word got out through my new friend Judy. I wasn't familiar with her last name and missed blocking her from the notifications. She publicly announced how excited she was to read my book, told others about it, and posted a review on Amazon.com.

My fears had been unnecessary. The experience allowed Judy and I to be great friends in a short amount of time. She is not the only one. I have far deeper friendships now that I have laid all my cards on the table. The book has given others the courage to open up as well. Sometimes I think we just need someone to go first and learn to recognize safe people.

My love and gratitude always go to my husband and best friend, Scott. Sometimes I wish we would have met earlier in life, but it would never have worked. We needed to become our current selves for it to be this good. You are my "split-apart."

Thank you to Judy Parkins, Certified Life Coach, for bringing your expertise in writing engaging and reflective questions for the reader and for always making me laugh.

Special thanks to Catherine Lennox of Write Contact for working through my content for clarification in my books and always encouraging me.

Prison Fellowship Regional Director Mark Hubbell is in a class by himself. Your selflessness in helping me and my mission through the years is inspiring. I have difficulty fathoming the level of commitment you hold for sharing the love of God to the incarcerated. Knowing that hundreds of my books offer hope and encouragement to inmates through your contact network is heartwarming. You and Deb are dear to me, and I thank you.

Words fail me in describing the gratitude and admiration I feel for business coach Patti Cotton and publishing coach Patrick Snow. To have both accomplished so much in your respective fields and maintained the generous hearts of serving others is astounding. Your guidance and thought-provoking have made me a better communicator and stretched me as a writer.

I am grateful for my counselors and therapists as the work continues, but they shall remain anonymous since that falls under doctor-patient confidentiality.

ABOUT THE AUTHOR

TERESA NICKELL is an author, professional speaker, life coach, and volunteer with Prison Fellowship and recovery centers. She is a master storyteller who connects to her audience with a humble, candid, gritty style that makes her easily relatable. Her speaking and writing are direct and authentic; they offer a hope-filled approach to very difficult subject matter. Teresa lives with her husband Scott and two little misfit dogs in rural Idaho.

Teresa can be reached through her website. She is available for select speaking engagements and coaching. Your Amazon reviews are greatly appreciated.

www.TeresaNickell.com

Follow Teresa on Facebook at The Girl in Your Wallet

God, please help me set aside everything I think I know about myself, my circumstances, my future, and especially You, for an open mind about myself, my circumstance, my future, and especially You.